Life in an Old
New England Country Village

Life in an Old New England Country Village

An OLD
STURBRIDGE
VILLAGE Book

Catherine Fennelly

THOMAS Y. CROWELL COMPANY   NEW YORK   ESTABLISHED 1834

Designed by Barbara Kohn Isaac

Manufactured in the United States of America

L.C. Card 69-18668

2 3 4 5 6 7 8 9 10

ISBN 0-690-49093-3

Material from the following Village publications by the author has been used in this volume:
Old Sturbridge Village: A Guidebook
The New England Village Scene: 1800
The Country Lawyer in New England, 1790–1840
Town Schooling in Early New England, 1790–1840

Photographs, unless otherwise credited, are from Old Sturbridge Village and were taken by James C. Ward and Russell C. Hamilton.

To the memory of the three men—
Albert Bacheller Wells,
Joel Cheney Wells,
and George Burnham Wells—
whose vision first contemplated and
mapped out Old Sturbridge Village,
and to all the others who have
helped complete it.

Foreword

Life in an Old New England Country Village is a book about New England in the early part of the nineteenth century. It is, in a sense, a social history—but with a difference, for the life and times of the New Englander as described herein are in fact as portrayed by Old Sturbridge Village, a living museum of early New England that has re-created an agricultural community of a century and a half ago.

This is not a casual re-creation. It has not been based upon sentiment for the past, nor upon a sense of what is right aesthetically. Rather, it has been based upon the record—the result of careful documentary research, architectural evidence, and a study of the domestic artifacts, arts, and village industry of the period. It is the result of a large investment of both time and talent by a dedicated staff of specialists, motivated by the belief that the time, the place, and the people represented here have made major contributions to American life and that a knowledge of that heritage gives a sense of meaning and direction to our lives.

Old Sturbridge Village is a nonprofit, educational institution. Annual attendance is approaching the three-quarters-of-a-million mark. Growth has been unusually rapid and has early led the Village to accept its rightful responsibility as an outdoor history museum and an educational institution to share its resources and its knowledge with a public of infinitely varied social and educational backgrounds. It has led to the exercise of sound scholarship in the many forms of interpretation needed to assist visitors to discover relationships between historical themes and three-dimensional objects, and to form meaningful judgments from their firsthand experience. It has led the Village into close cooperation with formal educational institutions—the public schools from whence come more than 75,000 children in classes each year, whose studies are enriched and whose understandings are deepened by the Village's school program; and the colleges and universities with whom jointly sponsored courses, teacher workshops, seminars, and special tours are conducted. It has also led to specialized interpretation for special interest groups such as antiques collectors, historical organizations, and those interested in early industry, crafts, or tools.

And so, this volume may be considered a further extension of that interpretation and, indeed, of the underlying purpose of Old Sturbridge Village—to preserve and present the story of New England farm and village life of yesterday, and to impart a knowledge and understanding of that heritage for the cultural enrichment of the citizens of today.

Alexander J. Wall, President

OLD STURBRIDGE VILLAGE

Contents

Introduction   1

1. The New England Village   13

2. The Farm   19

3. The Meetinghouses   35

4. The Candia Schoolhouse   53

5. The Law Office   65

6. The Tavern   85

7. The Village Center   111

    Miner Grant's General Store   111

    The Bank   118

    The Printing Office   123

8. The Shops and Mills   129

    The Blacksmith Shop   129

    The Cabinet Shop   130

    The Pewterer's Shop   132

The Tinsmith Shop   133

The Broommaker Shop   135

The Pottery Shop   136

The Cooperage   138

The Gristmill   138

The Sawmill   142

The Carding Mill   144

9. The Residences   149

The John Fenno House   155

The Fitch House   160

The Richardson House   167

The Salem Towne House   171

The Collections   185

Conclusion   191

Index   205

Life in an Old
New England Country Village

The Village Green after a snowfall.

Introduction

"When I die you will find engraved upon my heart 'New England.'" These haunting words of Thomas Hutchinson, the last royal governor of the province of Massachusetts Bay, penned in exile to a friend as he grieved for the land he loved, echo poignantly through the centuries to present-day lovers of the New England scene. And New England *is* loved, perhaps more for what it was than for what it is, perhaps blindly and with little perspective by many of its champions, but generally with such warmth and fondness that people return to it again and again. They may never want to live there, for the climate is more bracing than clement, but they are attracted by its aura of past greatness, a half-forgotten memory of an age when high principles were taken for granted, and man lived close to nature and to God.

We of the mid-twentieth century like to think our characterization on the pages of history will be that of concern—that we strove to make a better life for all Americans and, beyond that, for the world. Young people especially have taken to themselves all the cares of humanity; they are fired with a sense of justice and equality, if not of tolerance. Perhaps they too will be drawn back to a day more than a century and a half ago when the humanitarian impulse was first making itself felt in New England, when men began to understand that they had an obligation to work for universal education, for extension of the system of higher education, for reform of prisons and of the poor law, for better care for the deaf, the blind, and the insane. Eventually that broad stream of humanitarianism was to narrow and focus on the abolition of slavery, the consequences of which have led directly to the greatest domestic problem of the mid-twentieth century.

The New England of 1800 or even as late as 1840 presented an idyllic picture of a region blessed by nature with a fine coastline, broad rivers, rushing streams, still abundant forests in its northern and western reaches, good farmland along its rivers, adequate rainfall, prosperous towns and villages, and an energetic people. It was in the early stages of an industrial revolution that was to change it physically as well as mentally and emotionally, and it had yet to experience the great influx of European immigration that was almost to engulf it a few years later. It was still largely agricultural and was only beginning to awaken to the problems of transportation, communications, and supply that the large cities would create. Its population was homogeneous: no need as yet to consider the plight of the tenement dweller, the non-English-speaking, the factory slave, the street urchin, or the man of different color. Rather was it concerned with protecting its burgeoning industry and commerce in a nation as yet largely agricultural, with fitting its economy into that of the nation, with populating its northern and western lands, expanding its markets, and investing wisely in the new industry and communications.

In our sometimes blind groping for a way out of today's dilemmas this view of New England in the early nineteenth century appeals to our sense of serenity and order. These New Englanders lived in a quieter, more secure world than ours, but both their clear-eyed view of their own society and its needs and their vision for the future of America remind us that the bond is closer than we think.

The New England scene, however, was not all peace and security. In addition to the problems of adjusting to a new nation and a new society, New Englanders had themselves to contend with. Their very virtues had a darker side. If these people were steadfast, devoted to their region and its welfare, they were also provincial, suspicious of foreigners and new ideas, intolerant of anyone who thought differently or lived differently.

Their frugality occasionally resulted in penuriousness and a refusal to enjoy life. The very peacefulness of the countryside, the solitude, the hard work, and the demands of the Puritan ideal too often were more than body and soul could bear, with the result that excessive drinking was perhaps the greatest social problem of the day. Every age pays the price of its ideals, and early nineteenth-century New England was no exception.

But because these people lived as they did, thought as they did, and acted as they did, Old Sturbridge Village exists today,

The pond and river from the Towne House garden.

not just as a memorial to them but as a bridge between them and the present. One can turn off U.S. Route 20 or 84, cross the town bridge, and within moments find oneself back in time a hundred and sixty-odd years in the heart of a rural New England community.

The settlement at Old Sturbridge Village represents the achievement of two brothers, Albert B. and Joel Cheney Wells. They were sons of a Southbridge, Massachusetts, industrial magnate who brought up his three boys on a farm, sent them to local schools, and then on to preparatory school and college. All three entered their father's business, the American Optical Company, rose through the ranks, and ended their business careers as its officers and directors. Albert, known as A.B., and Joel Cheney traveled extensively on this continent and in Europe. Both were interested in history. Albert, with a keenly practical mind, discovered that his preference was for inventions and materials. Joel Cheney was impressed by fine workmanship and beauty of line and color.

The covered bridge.

Family tradition relates that Albert, vacationing in Vermont
in the late 1920's and prevented by heavy rain from playing his
anticipated round of golf, was persuaded by a friend to go
antique hunting with him instead. The result was that he became an avid collector. Joel Cheney began collecting at almost
the same time, generally limiting his field of interest to clocks
and paperweights. Albert collected the tools of agriculture and
industry, the simpler furnishings of farm households, the contents of barns and shops. He was fascinated by materials as well
as by tools and gadgets. In his search for woodenware he traveled
to Great Britain, sending home burl bowls, English Windsor
chairs, Welsh love spoons, and other treen. From Spain he sent
fine examples of the ironmaster's craft—andirons, spits, lanterns, candelabra, racks, and hooks—and hand-blown, engraved, and painted glassware. He also collected in the Southwest, where he developed an interest in Indian crafts. Early
visitors to Old Sturbridge Village were intrigued by the collections of woodenware, children's toys, Schimmel and other Penn-

The woodland walk.

sylvania Dutch carvings, chalkware, weathervanes, wrought iron, mechanical devices ranging from mousetraps to laundry equipment, northern European copper and brass, southern European faïence, along with sickles, scythes, reapers, winnowers, and the many tools of agriculture, and the blacksmith's, farrier's, carpenter's, and cabinetmaker's tools. Many of these collections have since been weeded out, refined, and brought into relation to the period and area of the present Village.

At first A. B. kept his collections in his own home, but they soon overflowed into basement, barns, outbuildings, office, and homes of friends. Joel Cheney placed many of his clocks in the offices of the American Optical Company. A.B.'s wife, Ethel Burnham Wells, found herself crowded out of her home and was naturally somewhat dismayed. She must later have remembered the old maxim "If you can't lick 'em, join 'em" because she eventually contributed substantially to the project. A. B. enjoyed showing his collection to interested friends and soon set up a series of exhibit rooms. Finally the storage and display problems became acute; there was no more room for what he had, much less for the contents of the station wagons, trucks, and wagons that arrived almost weekly with new additions to the collections. Clearly something had to be done.

George Burnham Wells, A. B.'s son, had lived with the collections for some years, had inherited his father's interest in history—although it was English rather than American history that attracted his attention—and felt strongly that the collections should be put to some purpose. The idea of a formal museum did not appeal to him. He felt that the collections would mean much more to the American people if they could be seen in their natural setting, and he urged his father and uncle to display their treasures as they had once been used—in a farm, shop, or home setting—so that they could tell their story directly to those who would come to see. Thus it was George Burnham Wells who was directly responsible for the Village as it exists today.

Thus was the ideal born. At the instigation of George Burnham Wells and with the help of others, notably Elliott Clemence and Russell Kettel—land was purchased in nearby Sturbridge. Here lay a 250-acre tract of meadow, woodland, river, and millpond, all of it once farm or mill property, a near-perfect setting for the re-creation of a farm community of 1790–1840. Here was space for gristmill, sawmill, and finishing mill, for shops and homes, for farm and for meetinghouse, for schoolhouse and printing office. Next best to restoring a village that once had been was creating one on land that once had been so used, bringing back to it the kinds of structures it had or might have had, creating a bit of New England's past out of New England present.

With the acquisition of the property in 1936, 1937, and 1938 came a search for buildings to occupy it. Already present were three houses built in the late eighteenth century—the Oliver Wight House, a cottage near it, and the old Gate House—three shops which were later to become the woodworking shop, tin

The Carding Mill in South Waterford, before its removal to Old Sturbridge.

shop, and boot shop, a barn at the Wight House, and a carriage house near the Gate House.

First a dam had to be constructed to restrain the Quinebaug River and protect the millpond. Then the first building was brought in, a sawmill from Gilead, Connecticut. Next came a barn from Schoharie, New York, a gristmill from Hebron, Connecticut, houses from Willimantic, Connecticut, and East Brookfield, Massachusetts, and a store from Stafford, Connecticut. A gun shop, a spectacle shop, a blacksmith shop, a blacksmith's and a miller's house, and a wagon shed were built, largely from old timber and all of them copies or adaptations of old structures. The Wells brothers, with architectural assistance, drew up the plans, which called for a central common or green with houses and shops around and radiating from it. This is essentially the layout of the Village Green today.

The Village was inaugurated as Quinabaug Village Corporation, later Old Sturbridge Inc., on July 15, 1938. The collections comprised the Wells Historical Museum, which eventually was merged with Old Sturbridge Inc. The purpose of the Village at first was twofold: to maintain and exhibit "a model village" for the education of the public and to train apprentices in New England arts and crafts. The second goal was later dropped.

One of the earliest interests at Old Sturbridge Village was in training craftsmen—teaching young men and women to know and appreciate the superb workmanship of the past and to adapt from and build on the past in perfecting their own styles. Eventually the idea of developing contemporary craftsmanship had to give way to the necessity of concentrating on one area only—early nineteenth-century New England. Thus the crafts shown at the Village today are those that were practised by New Englanders of that period, who had learned them from past generations, and who, in turn, expanded and improved upon them until by 1840 a good number were no longer household or small-shop crafts at all, but rather single steps in large industrial operations concentrated in a factory system.

The Second World War interrupted the museum's progress. New construction ceased, many of the staff were called to other labors, and only a few were left to attend to essential duties. Some work on the collections continued, but eventually even that had to be suspended.

As soon as the war was over, construction began again. A

Rebuilding the mill raceway.

cabinet shop and schoolhouse (for exhibition of the clock collection) were next erected. The curator returned and began
again working on the collections and preparing exhibitions for
the buildings. By early summer 1946 all was ready and the
Village formally opened to the public on June 8. Eighty-nine
visitors passed through that day, and the first season ended
with a total attendance of 5,170. Comparison with the figure
of some 578,000 for 1968 will give an idea of the growth over
a twenty-two year period.

Every New England community that had direct communica-
tion with other towns, was on a stage route—or even had inhabitants who demanded some entertainment away from home

in the evening—had a tavern. Thus the next building to be erected was an inn, and because visitors to the Village must be fed and several exhibits housed, it was decided to erect a frankly made-up tavern, with modern kitchens and rest rooms but recapturing as much as possible the air of the old hostels. Now the need for a meetinghouse became acute. Fortunately a fine old Baptist meetinghouse was found in nearby Fiskdale; it was moved in and placed at the head of the Green, where it both dominates and gives coherence and unity to the Village plan.

In 1948 a candlemaker's shop was erected and opened, and work began on the Mashapaug House, later to be a textile exhibition and demonstration building, and on a pottery shop. The Pliny Freeman Farmhouse was acquired in 1950 and moved to the Village in 1951. It was opened to the public in 1952, along with the Isaiah Thomas Printing Office, the Fenno House, the Lincoln House, the Dummerston Covered Bridge, and the Herb Garden. A sales building, Handcraft House, had been opened the previous year.

By 1954 a Quaker meetinghouse had been moved in from Bolton, Massachusetts. A pound for stray animals and a powder house were next set up. Then in late summer 1955 came a disastrous flood resulting from hurricane-caused rain. For a brief time the future of the Village looked black indeed, but then hundreds of its friends rallied to its support and contributed the more than $100,000 needed for repair and reconstruction. Federal flood control measures meant that the farm unit, badly flooded out and in part washed off its foundation, would have to be moved. It was relocated on higher ground, on a hill overlooking its own fields, and reopened in 1957. The blacksmith shop, destroyed by fire in the winter of 1956, was replaced by a stone shop from Bolton. In 1957 the breathtakingly beautiful gift of J. C. Wells and his wife, the Salem Towne House, was opened at one end of the Green, opposite the Meetinghouse, and its lovely garden, enchanting view of the millpond, and fine old barn completed the Green. But two more buildings, a small lawyer's office and a bank, wells, outhouses, barns, and fences remained to be installed in this area.

In the early 1960's a schoolhouse, new pottery shop, and bake house were erected. Later a carding mill was acquired in Maine, and quite recently a second store has been found in

Dummerston, Vermont, and a cooper's shop in Waldoboro, Maine. There are plans for adding a dwelling in the Greek Revival architectural style, a mill-house unit, a doctor's office, a textile mill, and perhaps a few other stores and shops.

But physical appearance is not enough. The Village staff has striven constantly and valiantly to evoke the very life of the community—the sights, smells, even the feeling of the past. Hosts, hostesses, and demonstrators are costumed in the dress of the period. The ox-cart, the chaise, and the wagon drive around the Green and along the road leading to the mills just as they would have long ago. A puppet show near the Tavern reminds one that this form of entertainment was once frowned on, and the dramatic re-enactment going on in the Meetinghouse, itself not authentic, gives the audience some insight into

Installing a new wheel at the Gristmill.

the minds and hearts of our forebears. The scent of freshly baked "plumb" cake wafts out from the Bake House door, and the chiming of clocks at the Clock Shop, the beat of the press in the Printing Office, the blow of the hammer at the blacksmith's forge, and the clank of the carding mill all are the sounds of 1830 and 1840.

The New England Village   1

By the opening of the nineteenth century the five states of New England were made up of a series of townships. (Maine, the sixth state in the region, was admitted to the Union in 1820.) Each township was composed of one, two, or a series of villages—small hamlets or larger towns—surrounded by open farmland, woodland, marsh in some areas, and often wasteland. The village within the township was essentially a self-sufficient community, with meetinghouses, schoolhouses, taverns, stores, shops, perhaps a factory or two, often a post office, sometimes an academy, and, if the town happened to be a county seat, a courthouse and jail. A typical village might have a population of fifty families, but the population of the town itself might be 2,000 or more. If the village was located on a stream with a good flow, there would be a gristmill, a sawmill, and perhaps one or two other industries requiring water power. The blacksmith was essential to the community, as was the miller and the keeper of the general store.

Early travelers left innumerable descriptions of these villages. Many remarked on the houses gleaming with paint, the beautifully tended gardens, or the happy and healthy children on their way to school, but others noted that the houses seemed small and crowded, doorways and streets ill-kept, and that neglect was frequently visible. The Reverend Timothy Dwight, president of Yale, noted on his travels a "style of building neat

and tidy. Fences and outhouses are also in the same style, and being almost universally painted white, make a delightful appearance to the eye; an appearance not a little enhanced by the great multitude of shade trees." In another town he found "lots universally covered with a rich verdure and adorned with flourishing orchards." Henry Wansey, an English textile manufacturer, observed that village houses were

generally built after the following mode: a framed work of timber, weatherboarded and roofed with shingles, two-storey high, besides the attic, a good cellar beneath with three steps up into the house, two windows on each side of the door, five in the next storey, all sashed, and the whole neatly painted; some of a free stone color, others white with green doors and window shutters. The women and children in most of the country places go without caps, shoes, or stockings.

The New Haven green, about 1790. Painting by William Giles Munson.
(New Haven Colony Historical Society)

The houses in rural villages were usually simple wooden structures, although an occasional house was of brick and a rare one of stone. If the town had been settled early, there probably were a few houses surviving from the seventeenth century, and these resembled the English houses of the same period, though usually they were fully timbered instead of half-timbered. But most had been built in the eighteenth century—salt boxes, with a long, slanting roof at the rear, two-story square structures, or one- or two-room cottages. The newest houses were Federal or Greek Revival in style, with classical lines, balanced proportions, and light and airy interiors. Thus Lyman Beecher's wife, when she first saw Litchfield, Connecticut, in 1817, remarked on the beauty of the wide streets, the green in the center of town, the handsome buildings including meeting-

New Bedford, Massachusetts, in 1807. Lithograph of a painting by William A. Wall. (New-York Historical Society, New York City)

house, courthouse, tavern, and bank, the fine trees, and the clean white paint on the houses. Her stepdaughter, Harriet Beecher Stowe, loved the deep dooryards, the large side gardens, the beds of scarlet peonies, the white and yellow lilies, and long-branching trees. Foreigners were more aware of the shops along the main street—"cabinetmakers, shoemakers, saddlers, cordmakers, and tanners"—the neat and airy look of the villages as a whole, the white churches with their tall spires, the green shutters on white houses, the surprising number of windows in each dwelling, the fine orchards and fields. The people who inhabited these gleaming houses were mostly farmers, and indeed most men farmed at least part time.

John Adams felt that the meetinghouse, schoolhouse, and military training field were "the scenes where New England men are formed," and every New England village had all three institutions. The leaders of the community were the clergymen, ministers of the Congregational, Unitarian, Episcopal, and Baptist churches. One or two wealthy merchants or landowners, the justice of the peace, and perhaps a prominent attorney might be entitled to use "Esquire" after their names, and they were the social and political leaders of the community, the squires. The independent farmers came next in the social scale, with perhaps the storekeepers, the blacksmith, and the more prosperous mill owners and artisans. Next came the farm laborers, mechanics, less prosperous artisans, house servants, Indians, and former slaves. The social structure was fairly rigid, but all classes mixed in the meetinghouse, at town meeting, and often in social intercourse. A neighbor's son doing seasonal work in the fields or a daughter helping out in the house was considered a social equal and as a matter of course sat at the family table. A quilting or spinning bee in the home, or a house raising, a field-clearing stone bee, or an ox pull among the men drew together all classes for an afternoon or evening of work and entertainment, just as did the meetinghouse for worship and discussion on the Sabbath. Children of all classes mingled in the district school, and their teacher was most often a local farmer's daughter or son who wished to become a minister and who needed to earn a few dollars between terms at the academy or at Harvard or Yale.

Although its social structure was fairly rigid, the New England village was not unchanging. If a few families controlled the governorship, the upper house of the legislature, and the judiciary in most of the states, it was still possible for others to break into their circle by virtue of talent, education, profession, and sometimes wealth or marriage. The attraction of western and northern lands in Ohio and Illinois, in Maine and Vermont, drew off much of the population of the villages, with the result that the census figures for 1810, 1820, and 1830 often showed the older settlements stationary if not actually declining in population. The lure of industry also drew off young people to work in commercial towns and in the mills. The result, until the mass immigration from Ireland and western Europe, was a fairly homogeneous society made fluid by emigration and broadened in its outlook by the rise of industry, the building of the railroad, and the growth of markets for

South view of Pittsfield, New Hampshire, in the 1850's. Lithograph by J. B. Bachelder.

agriculture. All this was to change in the 1840's and 1850's, but until then New England was still the "garden of villages" commented on and admired by every traveler, even by those who deplored the conservatism, provincialism, and rigid morality of its inhabitants.

Augusta, Maine, in the 1850's, drawn by F. B. Ladd. Lithograph printed by F. Heppenheimer.

The Farm

2

At the opening of the nineteenth century more than ninety percent of all New Englanders were farmers, and that percentage did not change radically until after 1840. Although there was some industry and commerce, particularly along the coast, and the people seemed to have an inborn mechanical bent, most of them were farmers first of all.

On the outskirts of the few cities and large towns, in the river valleys, and even in the rocky uplands, New Englanders grazed their cattle, tilled their fields, harvested their crops and prepared them for market. Until the railroads were able to develop and tap the grain-growing regions of the Midwest, New England towns were fed largely by the New England countryside. Rye, oats, Indian corn, cheese, butter, hay, horses, cattle, and sheep were shipped out of the region to New York, Philadelphia, Baltimore, Charleston, the West Indies, and Europe. Even though New England's export crops did not compare in quantity with those of New York, Pennsylvania, or the southern states, they were considerable, and they represented the chief economy of the region.

The face of New England in 1800 was covered with hundreds of small towns and villages, each with its surrounding farms. Nearly every adult male did some farming, no matter whether his vocation was that of clergyman, lawyer, merchant, or artisan. The farmer usually owned some acres of land, and the arable acres he farmed. If farming was his chief occupation, he belonged to the vast economic majority.

The typical New England farm of the early nineteenth century comprised fifty to two hundred acres. Only part of the land was in tilled fields. The rest was meadow, pasture, woodland, orchard, and waste. In the fields were grain crops—notably Indian corn, wheat, rye, oats, and buckwheat—with occasional small plots of turnips, pumpkins, and carrots. Hemp and flax were grown where there was sufficient moisture. In the kitchen garden the farm wife raised small vegetables and herbs for the family—beans and carrots, mint, rosemary, sage, and tansy. In the larger garden were grown watermelon, potatoes, sweet corn, cabbage, squash, pole beans, peas, and onions. For a brief time hops were a profitable crop in some areas, as was broomcorn

The Pliny Freeman Farm in winter.

in Hampshire County, Massachusetts. Onions were harvested for export in the Wethersfield-Windsor areas of Connecticut, and tobacco was grown in both these regions.

Every industrious farmer kept a pair of oxen for heavy hauling, stone and stump pulling, harrowing and ploughing. Usually he also had a team of horses. Six to a dozen cows, twelve or fourteen sheep, a few pigs, geese, and other barn-yard fowl completed his livestock. (Just before and imme-diately after the War of 1812 there was a speculative boom in Merino sheep, but this soon died out. Other breeds were raised profitably in Vermont in the 1820's and 1830's.) Barn and house cats fought a constant battle against the rodents that threatened to engulf both structures, and every farm family had a dog. A few farmers had mules, which they raised for market. Many communities kept a town bull to service the cows allowed to graze on the common. This practise was dying out, however, as more and more towns enacted bylaws forbidding creatures to roam at large.

Because agriculture was New England's chief industry, be-cause it was a small-scale industry, and because most rural New Englanders were farmers, the farm unit is perhaps the most important in the entire Village. The Pliny Freeman farm-stead is in microscope a reconstruction of a New England farm of 1820 or so. It has the obvious limitations of its location—salt hay and cranberries, for instance, cannot be grown along the Quinebaug. It is not new farmland, nor could it be in an area already settled for nearly a century in 1820. It will never grow tobacco well, perhaps never will have an outstanding wheat crop, and will have great difficulty in reverting cattle and sheep to the scrawny, undersized (by today's standards) breeds of an earlier day. Its methods of cultivation, its fertil-izers, its crops, and its layout are those of the earlier day. Its fields have been telescoped to fit within a few acres what would normally have been spread out over eighty or more.

The Pliny Freeman Farmhouse was built in the town of Sturbridge in 1801. Pliny Freeman's father, Comfort, built it for him. Here Pliny brought his bride, reared seven children, and struggled to make a living for his family. In a small shop on his farm he made ox bows, which he traded in at the store or sent to market. Either he was not very successful or his

The farm kitchen.

ambitions were greater, or both, for within a few years he drifted west into New York State. Eventually he returned to Massachusetts. He died in Webster in 1855.

The Farmhouse stood on what is now Route 15 and 84; in 1949, when the Commonwealth of Massachusetts condemned the land to make way for this highway, Old Sturbridge Village purchased the house for the sum of one dollar and moved it. In 1951 it was re-erected in the Village meadowland, not far from the Quinebaug River. Its entire frame was moved on a cradle across the river. The Farmhouse was opened to visitors in 1952. In 1955 it was badly damaged by flood and had to be moved. Two years later the unit was reopened on its present site.

Today the Farmhouse stands on a hill overlooking lower-lying farmland and meadow, the millpond and bridge, the Carding Mill, the Blacksmith Shop, and the Tinsmith and Broomaker shops. The fields and meadow are below and in front, woodland and high pasture in the rear. Above the pasture is so much hilly rock as to be waste for many years to come—despite current efforts to clear it; beyond it is more

22

The farmhouse buttery.

land capable of cultivation. On either side of the house are the herb and kitchen gardens. The large barn is to one side; sheep shed, vehicle shed, barn, smokehouse, and shop are at the rear. The farmyard is filled with snow and ice in winter, deep in mud in the spring, dry and dusty in summer and early fall.

The Pliny Freeman Farmhouse must have been badly crowded when the seven children were all living at home. The family entered it, as would any farm family, through the kitchen door, leading from the barn and yard. In bad weather, one could come in through the shed. In the shed and ell extension were all the gear not stored in the barn: traps for hunting, snowshoes and skates, grain sieve, winnower, buckets, pails and spigots used in tapping the maple trees, flour and sugar barrels, axes, shovels, other tools, and firewood brought inside to dry. Whole cords of wood were piled outside the house every fall, ready for chopping and bringing in. In an age when the only heat was that of the fireplace, which was cooking stove and hot-water heater as well, many farmers were hard put to it to keep their woodland sufficiently well forested to supply their annual needs.

The kitchen and buttery were the working areas of the house. To the tasks we know today—preparing meals three times a day, cleaning, laundering, ironing, mending, and supervising small children—the farm wife added candle and soap making, wool and flax combing and carding, spinning, weaving, dyeing yarn and cloth, making sausages, baking bread, occasionally brewing beer or assisting in bottling cider, drying herbs and fruits, pickling and preserving, tending her vegetable and kitchen garden, and acting as kindergarten, first grade, and Sunday school teacher. She rose long before dawn on winter mornings, with the sun in early summer, and she put aside her knitting or mending only at the evening curfew hour of nine. This was not an age when women gave much thought to retaining their youth. They were married at twenty or earlier, produced large families when they did not die young in childbirth or of consumption, and knew nothing of the need to use their leisure wisely. They had no leisure.

The farm housewife of 1800 or 1820 had no cookstove. Her first morning task was to revive the fire on the open kitchen hearth or start a new one. Then she sliced the bread, made coffee or tea, poured cornmeal into a pot of boiling water, and prepared the family breakfast of cornmeal mush, bread or toast, and a hot drink. Occasionally there was a bit of bacon or sausage for the adults, leftover potatoes fried up, or doughnuts. In some families there was pie. After the meal was cleared, the children had to be made ready for school, lunch baskets packed, the baby fed and washed. When the house was reasonably neat, beds made, and dinner under way, she could spare some time for spinning linen for sheets or weaving a web of broadcloth for a new coat for her husband.

Her noon meal most often was a boiled dinner—salted beef or pork boiled with potatoes, carrots, turnips, onions, and whatever else she chose to put into the pot. The cider mug was passed from hand to hand, for this was the traditional New England drink and every farmer cultivated his orchard, pressed his apples, made cider, and put it into the cellar in large barrels. In late winter or early spring he bottled it to keep it wholesome before the next season's pressing was ready. Dessert might be gingerbread, apple pie, or a baked Indian pudding.

One hopes that the farmer's wife was able to rest after the

noon dinner, but if so it was only in sitting down to nurse the baby, mend, or cut strips for carpeting. More likely she worked in her kitchen garden, returned to her loom or wheel, or got out her flat and goffering irons and pressed shirts, aprons, and table linen. Her evening meal was a simple supper,

The farm kitchen table set for noonday dinnner.

called tea, about five or six o'clock. Then came an evening of sewing, knitting, supervising the children in their school lessons, and family prayers before bedtime at nine o'clock.

True, this farm wife did not have to drive her children to and from school, work for the P.T.A., the League of Women Voters, or the local youth center. She did not have to worry about getting her children to music lessons, dancing lessons, Little League practice, the dentist, and the psychiatrist. She did laundry only biweekly or monthly, less often in winter. She did not feel she had to carpet-sweep or mop daily, and she was not called upon to entertain the bridge club or her husband's boss at the drop of a hat. But she did perform daily drudgery, worked incessantly, raised a large family if she was able, and endured the sorrow of losing young children. More often than not she was deeply religious; she knew that her duty was to rear her children in the love and fear of the Lord, and she set them daily an example of patience, courage, and hard work. Her love for them she did not display easily or lightly, but it was present in her every act and attitude.

Her husband was responsible chiefly for the acres he tilled —for his grains, his root crops, his flax and hops, and his orchard. He bred, milked, and pastured the cows. He found grazing for the sheep, sheared them in late spring or early summer, and kept them in warm sheds in winter. The fowl he usually left to his wife, but the care of the swine, the oxen, and the horses was his.

Planting, cultivating, fertilizing, and harvesting took long days of hard labor. In winter when he could not work in the fields he built and repaired fences, kept his harness in order, husked, threshed, flailed, and winnowed grain, bottled cider, repaired the house, sheds, and barns, shoveled and ploughed snow on paths and roads, cut wood endlessly, and did the hundreds of other chores necessary to a rural economy. Evenings he spent keeping his accounts, oiling and cleaning his gun, doing small tasks that could be performed within the family circle.

Occasionally there were visitors or overnight guests—perhaps relatives come for a visit, neighbors living at a distance, or travelers taken in as a matter of course. Then the whole family might participate in backgammon, checkers, or puzzle games, might take turns reading aloud from a new book of essays or verse, or engage in an impromptu songfest.

Farm children, once they got past the first two critical years when weaning, teething, scarlet fever, and diphtheria took a fearful toll, were generally healthy. They lived in the open air except for the three months in winter and few weeks in summer when they were forced to go to school to be "learned their letters." They were early taught to be useful around the house and outside. Boys helped their fathers in the lighter farmwork; girls assisted their mothers in the house and garden. Little girls of five and six were taught to knit; somewhat later they learned to spin, and as soon as their feet could reach the treadles they mastered the intricacies of weaving. Children

The trundle bed with quilted appliqué coverlet.

were then economic assets rather than liabilities to be financed through a long and expensive education.

The Freeman house is long and low, a simple box with a slanting roof, a long ell, and a shed at the rear. The main entrance is the kitchen door, since no housewife in her right mind would allow farm mud and grasses to be tracked into her parlor. The children were perhaps required to use the shed door. The kitchen usually was filled with aromas—the pleasant ones of baking bread or gingerbread, bubbling stew, or roasting meat; mundane ones of wax melting for candlemaking, apple slices and herbs drying before the fire, coffee beans roast-

The farm barn.

ing, or sausage being stuffed; or the unpleasant ones of the dyepot and its indigo mixture, the products of slaughtering, or milk souring for cheesemaking.

All the cooking was done at the large fireplace, where pots and kettles, toaster, waffle iron, oven peel, tin roaster, and all the other cooking paraphernalia were stored. On the mantel were pressing irons, candle molds, lamps, and other gear. The big table was used for both work and dining, and might have been set with a handloomed linen cloth, blue Staffordshire ware, white napery, and bone-handled knives and forks, as it is today. One suspects that the housewife did not always use

Merino sheep.

a cloth when there were no guests, but if she was fastidious she frequently did at noon.

The cupboards contained all the necessary kitchen equipment. Beyond them on one side is the buttery, where much food preparation took place. Here the housewife churned her butter, pressed and cared for her cheeses, kneaded her dough, stirred up her 'lection cakes (special yeast cakes made for Election Day), put up her preserves, and filled her pie shells and bean pot.

The door on the other side of the kitchen fireplace leads to the shed, filled with laundry equipment, skates and snowshoes, axes and shovels and brooms, and cords of wood.

The long ell-room between kitchen and shed housed seasonal equipment when not in use—a baby walker outgrown by the three-year-old and not yet needed by the current infant, spare pots and kettles brought out during the harvest season when there were extra mouths to feed, wool and flax waiting to be spun and dyed, and anything else not at the moment in use in the kitchen or buttery.

The parlor beyond the kitchen was what we today would perhaps call a "status symbol," necessary to preserve an aura of respectability so dear to every God-fearing New England housewife and never to be lightly entered. In the words of one contemporary writer it was never opened "except for the solemnization of a marriage or the obsequies of the dead." In spite of the sober dignity of its use, however, this room is gay with stenciled walls, a rag carpet, and colorfully stitched fringed curtains. Its fine desk, chest, and sewing table reflect some taste and prosperity on the part of the farmer. It was an awesome room to children, who had to be on their best behavior, with clean hands and wearing their best clothing, when they entered it.

There are three bedrooms in the Freeman Farmhouse, although only one is ordinarily shown. The downstairs chamber was the bedroom of the farmer and his wife. Under the bedstead is a trundle bed, where the current toddler and youngest child slept. This was a convenient arrangement when the child was croupy; his mother could hear him instantly. Experience had probably taught her to keep a kettle of hot water on the hearth for such emergencies. Behind the parlor fireplace is

The watering trough.

The corn barn.

room for a small clothes closet, unusual in farmhouses of the early nineteenth century. The upstairs chambers, not open to visitors, housed the rest of the family.

The front door of the farmhouse was opened only on formal occasions. Here, before walking down the path, today's visitor can look down upon the open fields and pasture, the mills and shops, millpond and river. One can sense here if nowhere else the dichotomy that was New England in the early years of the nineteenth century: a region poised on the brink of a tremendous industrial explosion yet still living in an age of agriculture, as unaware of its technological future as of the vast problems that industry would entail—the rapidly growing towns and cities, the exodus from the countryside, the pressure to find new markets at home and abroad, the need for a labor force and the consequences of immigration, the passing of agricultural predominance to the west. New England after 1830 would never be the same; it was caught helplessly, almost unwillingly, in the toils of the Industrial Revolution.

The Quaker Meetinghouse.

The Meetinghouses   3

If one had to choose a single symbol representative of New England in the early nineteenth century, he would probably settle on the meetinghouse—stark, often white, standing on a small rise and dominating both the town and its inhabitants. And indeed it did dominate the lives of most New Englanders of that day. As a public meetinghouse it served as town hall and civic auditorium, as well as church. Until the town built a hall all town meetings were held here, as were local, state, and federal elections. Here or in the tavern the selectmen met, bylaws were passed, town officers reported on the execution of their duties, and occasional justice courts were held. In the town meetings and in taking their turn at serving for a year or two as highway surveyor, fence viewer (checking for needed repairs), pound keeper, or hog reeve (guarding against strays), New Englanders gained an experience in self-government that was to serve them well in state and national affairs.

The meetinghouse was even more important as a place of public worship. Among the first buildings to be erected in any community, the meetinghouse and its religious ideal cast an overwhelming and permanent shadow on the minds and hearts of New Englanders. Its theology dominated their schools and colleges; it entered every home and impressed every life with a stamp that was forever to set off New Englanders from the rest of the nation.

The Village Meetinghouse began its existence in 1832 as the second Baptist Meetinghouse of Sturbridge. It was moved first to nearby Fiskdale and then, in 1947, to Old Sturbridge Village as the gift of the Baptist Association. It is Greek Revival in style, a country interpretation of this architectural vogue of the early nineteenth century. The stark whiteness of the exterior contrasts sharply with the interior, where the walls are a dull yellow, the ceiling a pale blue, and the pews, woodwork, and gallery painted in imitation oak graining. The style of the pews harks back to a slightly earlier age, but the pulpit is a mid-nineteenth-century mahogany structure. The pulpit and two of the chandeliers were still in the building when it was re-erected in the Village. The pews are a replacement. The organ, believed to have been made in Winchester, New Hampshire, comes from the Congregational Meetinghouse of West Lebanon, New Hampshire. The meetinghouse is used for Sunday afternoon Vesper services, a daily dramatic performance during the summer, Thanksgiving and Easter services, concerts, and meetings. Just as in the days of its youth, the building serves both secular and religious purposes.

The Quaker Meetinghouse, a gift of the Bolton, Massachusetts, Society of Friends, was erected in Bolton in 1796 at a cost of $945.14. To its length of thirty-four feet an additional twenty feet was added in 1818–1819 by the simple expedient of cutting the building through the center, pulling the two ends apart, and inserting the addition. The structure was restored to its original dimensions in 1953, after its removal to Old Sturbridge Village, where it now stands almost hidden among the pines that shelter it. The old pews, still intact, were simply stripped of later coats of paint. The clapboard exterior is painted its original gray. Inside the entry two doors, one for men and one for women, lead to the main body of the building and to the stairs to the three-sided gallery. The elders' benches face the congregation.

Below and to one side of the Village Meetinghouse is the graveyard, where the stones and markers of more than a century and a half ago attest to the New Englander's firm belief in the triumph of life after death. The stark stones, moved in from many places, reflect the simplicity of an age when the universal belief was that "man must suffer woe. Poverty may betide,

The Village Meetinghouse.

37

shame may arrest, pain may agonize, sorrow may sink, disease may waste, and death will befall." But man in the nineteenth century was learning that he must render to his fellow man as he rendered to God, compassion and service to the one, adoration and a blameless life to the other.

For almost two centuries before 1800 religion had dominated the lives of most New Englanders. Both the Pilgrims, or Separatists, who settled Plymouth, and the Puritans, who settled Salem, set up a series of individual churches that came to be known as Congregationalist. As they journeyed south and west into Connecticut and north into New Hampshire, and later into Maine and Vermont, they established these congregations. By the time of the American Revolution, Congregationalism was the dominant religion in the New England colonies. The Congregationalists frowned on the tolerance extended by Rhode Island to all sects, although in the Massachusetts Bay Colony and New Hampshire, where there were royal governors, the Church of England, or as we know it, the Episcopal Church, had to be given some rights of worship. There were many Baptists, but they had no rights in law, and the few scattered Quakers, Methodists, and Jews had only a handful of churches. There were almost no Catholics in New England before the immigration movements of the 1830's and 1840's.

Our ancestors were more conscious of the presence of God in their daily lives than are most of us today. Their ministers preached to them constantly of hell and damnation, of regeneration and predestination. Theirs was a stern God and a harsh religion, but it produced men and women who first carved out a territory for themselves, then wrested it from the power of Britain and established a new nation. Their religion was not democratic. In the earliest settlements the voting franchise was given only to church members, and a person could become a member only by undergoing and recounting to the meeting a genuine experience of religious conversion. This rigid requirement was modified by the Halfway Covenant late in the seventeenth century and by the Saybrook Platform of 1708. The Halfway Covenant permitted baptism of children of members, and the Saybrook Platform permitted admission to membership of all men and women of good lives who were sincerely desirous of salvation.

The tenets of colonial Congregationalism were based on Calvinism. God in His omniscience had determined that only the few were to be saved, and they were known as the elect of God. God must know that they were to be saved because He knows all things and He saves men of His own will. Thus developed the doctrines of denial of man's freedom of will, the salvation of the elect, and the damnation of the unrighteous. In all eternity God had foreordained some to be saved, the many to eternal punishment. So harsh and demanding a theology permitted those who were sure of salvation a clear conscience and a serene existence. The vast majority, however, lived in terror of damnation or developed a spirit of apathy and indifference. The society of the elect was exclusive indeed, and by the early eighteenth century there was general resentment of or indifference to the demands of rigid Congregationalism.

In the 1730's, however, there began in all the colonies a reaction, a reawakening of the religious impulse, an intensification of interest in things of the spirit that was to be known as the Great Awakening. The chief figure in New England's Great Awakening, and with Benjamin Franklin the possessor of one of the two finest minds in colonial America, was Jonathan Edwards, graduate of Yale, son and grandson of Congregationalist clergymen. Edwards preached mainly at his own church in Northampton, Massachusetts, but his books and sermons were read throughout the colonies. He condemned both the Halfway Covenant and Saybrook Platform as dangerous concessions to sinners and reinstated the membership requirement of a true religious experience. He preached of the wrath of God and the torment of hellfire with a passionate vividness seldom before heard in New England, but he taught also that those who are of the elect are free to walk in the path of righteousness and that the love of God is as sweet as His vengeance is awful. The emotional impact of Edwards' teaching, as that of the Awakening in general, was tremendous. But the fervor could not endure; the Awakening gradually subsided as people found themselves unable to sustain so high a pitch of religious exaltation, and in 1750 Edwards was dismissed from his parish. He had been opposed by the conservatives, led by Charles Chauncey of Boston, and increasingly by the radicals, the New Lights, many of whom formed independent churches or joined the Baptists.

New England Congregationalism achieved its greatest triumph in the Revolution. Almost without exception the clergy became patriot-preachers and spurred their congregations and the militia to greater efforts. Unconsciously they had been preparing the way for a long time, for the seeds of revolt against civil authority—unless it be also church authority—were implicit in Congregationalism. For more than a century its ministers had preached that God as well as man is bound by the immutable law of the universe and that God can no more violate that law than He can change His nature. Through Christ's atonement, God bequeathed this natural law to man, and under it the state as well as the individual is bound by compact. The purpose of all government is the common good, and no party to the compact may violate it with impunity. Liberty is the inheritance of man, and resistance to tyranny becomes a necessity. The path from nonresistance to noncompliance turned out to be not stony at all. As early as 1765 the preacher of the Massachusetts Bay election sermon stated flatly, "Submission to tyrannous rulers is so far from being a duty, that it is a crime. It is an offense against the state of which we are members, and whose happiness we ought to prefer to our chief joy; it is an offense against mankind, an offense against God."

With this background both clergy and laity, and regardless of what was happening among the Caucus of Boston or Sam Adams' Liberty Boys, were well prepared for revolution. To have remained Loyalist would have been to repudiate everything they had heard and learned from the pulpit since childhood. The Baptists wavered, but only briefly, and soon became full-fledged Patriots. Quakers, few as yet in number, took refuge in pacifism and nonresistance to both sides. Only the Anglicans experienced real difficulty. As members of the Church of England, they acknowledged the supremacy of George III over the church and prayed for the realm and the royal family each time they read the Book of Common Prayer. Many of them felt they had no choice but to remain loyal, and they either migrated or suffered at the hands of the Patriots.

As the clergy preached, so did they reap. Many Congregationalist ministers went off to serve as chaplains in the state militias. Others found their congregations decimated, abandoned wives and children in straitened circumstances, themselves and their flocks sometimes in the path of battling armies or marauding naval units. Little by little, as always in time of war, the laity began to take over. Thus the Westminster, Massachusetts, town meeting of 1778 would have startled the entire Ministerial Consociation had the ministers read its resolve:

The oftener power returns into the hands of the people the better, and when for the good of the whole the power is delligated, it ought to be done by the whole . . . Where can the power be lodged so well as they, or who has the boldness without blushing to say that the people are not suitable to putt in their own officers—if so why do we wast our blood and treasure to obtaine that which when obtained we are not fitt to enjoy, or if but a selected few only are fitt to appoint our rulers, why were we so uneasie under George?

That sentiment, as the clergy were soon to find out, could be turned on the church as well as the state.

The treaty of peace that ended the war with England was signed in 1783. The new world was indeed new. The Revolution had taken place in many spheres and on many levels and had brought with it the disruptions, the reallocations, the shiftings and changings that accompany and result from every war. For seven years the New England states had filled their quotas of militia, fed their armies, resisted invasion, and suffered raids and occupations. Many of the men who went off to the camps never returned; others came back wounded or maimed. Families had been broken. Country women had been forced to run the farms unaided or with the help of half-grown sons and neighbors. Orchards were untended, crops and soil neglected, livestock unimproved, houses and barns in disrepair. Roads had become overrun paths from lack of men to work on them. Commerce had been completely disrupted. Cut off from British and West India imports, both town and country had had to rely on their own produce. Self-sufficiency, as in any country where fighting is carried on on its own soil, had become the rule in every community.

A sharp rise in prices had brought about a disgraceful currency speculation. War profiteering, land grabbing, traffic in shoddy and illicit goods, high prices, the persecution of Loyalists, all resulted in a greatly lowered moral tone as the war

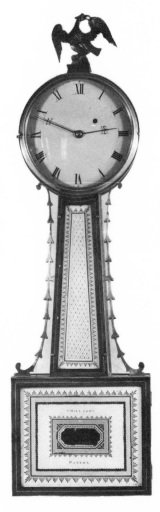

went on. Drinking and intemperance, according to the clergy, greatly increased. Women became freer in their manners. With fathers away in service, control over young people declined. Many towns felt they no longer could support the common schools, and thus school along with home discipline became lax or nonexistent.

Religion suffered as well. Along with the closing of churches, decimation of congregations, and general upheaval, there developed a growing impatience with the old order, a scorn for the ancient ways of Puritanism, an interest in new ideas and new philosophies. New theories were in the air—in government, in religion, and in social relations.

Of all the denominations, the Episcopal Church had been hardest hit by the war. At its end the church had to reorganize completely, achieve independence of the English church, secure resident bishops, and gain a legal position in the states. In 1784 the Reverend Samuel Seabury of Connecticut became the first resident bishop of the United States. By 1791 Connecticut had ten Episcopalian ministers, Massachusetts half that number. Episcopalians in Connecticut were outraged in 1791 when the state legislature passed an act enforcing the observance of days of public thanksgiving and fasting, for the Congregationalists in that state with grim humor annually arranged that thanksgiving should come on Good Friday and the fast day in Easter week. By the time of the adoption of the Connecticut Constitution of 1818 the state had close to a hundred Episcopal churches. These churches became objects of suspicion again in the War of 1812, but their growth was steady after that period. In 1823 Washington College, later Trinity, was chartered at Hartford for the training of their clergy.

The struggle of the Baptists for religious freedom took place in every state except Rhode Island, where they had had it almost from the beginning. They increased in great numbers. In Connecticut between 1760 and 1818 their societies increased from three to nearly a hundred. Many of the radical New Lights and stricter Congregationalists joined their fold. The Baptists would never be satisfied with mere religious toleration; what they demanded and eventually got was complete separation of church and state. Of all the New England churches they were the most democratic in their approach: their clergy were unlearned and of the people, their qualifications for church membership were lenient, and every member, including women, voted on church affairs. Rhode Island College, later Brown, became the first Baptist college in New England.

The growth of Methodism was slow in southern New England, rapid in the northern frontier regions. Most of New England in the late eighteenth and early nineteenth centuries was considered a mission area by this denomination. It had few established churches. Most of the preaching was done and conversions made by itinerant preachers on their circuits.

Quakers did not add greatly to their numbers during these years, but they did gain the complete religious freedom they had lacked so conspicuously in the seventeenth century. The Shaking Quakers, or Shakers, first appeared shortly before the Revolution. They settled in communities of their own, maintained a completely separate existence, refrained from marrying, and exercised little or no influence on the religious history of New England, though their communal life considerably influenced the thinking of New England utopians in the mid-nineteenth century.

In 1789 the storming of the Bastille in Paris was the signal for a general rejoicing in the United States that France was at last throwing off the remnants of royal despotism, of medieval law, religion, and education, and was about to embark on the same road taken earlier by this country—toward republican government, religious freedom, enlightened legislation, and universal free education. Overnight everything French became popular. Deism and the philosophies of the Enlightenment, already familiar to men of learning, became familiar to the common people as knowledge of their theories trickled down. The American religious foundation, already undermined by the impact of a revolution and its aftermath, came close to crumbling in the 1790's.

The challenge of revolutionary France was almost immediately evident to the New England clergy. The visions conjured up by the beheading of Louis XVI and his queen; by the blasphemous pagan spectacle at the Cathedral of Notre Dame in Paris—when a young girl was crowned Goddess of Liberty; by the Reign of Terror; and finally by the rise of Bonaparte seemed to the clergy and conservatives the challenge of Anti-

Christ to Christian civilization. Praises of the French experiment by men like Joseph Priestley and Thomas Paine and by the Republicans in this country were to the ministry the echoes of moral and political delusion. And when these same praises were reinforced by the new tenets of deism and infidelity to the church, it seemed to the older Congregationalists as though the United States and every decent principle it stood for were on the brink of destruction.

The religious problem of the 1790's was in large part political and social rather than theological. Practical New Englanders tended to correlate the new philosophy with laws of economics and the determination of social trends. If Europe was really disposed to cast out monarchy, splendid. If the world's material resources were inadequate to meet the needs of an ever increasing population, then surely the United States, and above all New England, was fittest to survive. If the purpose of government was to promote the greatest good of the greatest number, why in religion was there any validity to a doctrine of predestination, with its implicit exclusiveness? If every day in every way the world was becoming better and better, then each new event was but a step in development in this age of optimism. All things might yet be possible in this best of all possible worlds. The age of science, the age of reason, and the age of democracy, for in a limited sense it was that too, could not but question the old theology. The problem of the theologians was to create a body of thought that would seem new but depart little from the old.

Counterforces were already present in Connecticut and Massachusetts in the 1790's. Here a group of younger Congregationalist ministers closed ranks to form a group known as the New Divinity men, clerics devoted to the ancient faith and a strict discipline of its members. They initiated prayer meetings, special study groups, and lecture series in their churches and attacked from their pulpits backsliders, adherents of the new philosophy, and the philosophy itself. With renewed intensity and enthusiasm they recalled to their listeners the goodness of God and His promise of redemption. They denounced the godlessness of republican France, the unbridled democracy represented by Jefferson and the American Republicans, the licentiousness and immorality they were sure went hand in hand with belief in deism and freemasonry. As the minister at Ridge-field, Connecticut, put it: "About the time that Payne's Age of Reason came abroad, Infidelity presented itself to view, and like Milton's description of Death, 'black it stood at night fierce as ten furies, terrible as hell.' The horror in its features disgusted the people to such a degree that it has not as yet had one advocate in this town."

Partly as a result of these activities of the clergy, partly in reaction to several decades of religious indifference, and partly as a renewed expression of the Puritanism New Englanders would never completely throw off, there took place at the close of the eighteenth century and in the early decades of the nineteenth a series of religious revivals known as the Second Great Awakening. Beginning in such tiny hamlets as West Simsbury and Norfolk, Connecticut, and Beverly and Reading, Massachusetts, the revivals spread to the colleges and to the larger towns and were periodically repeated well into the 1830's. Nor were they Congregationalist only. There were also revivals among Episcopalians, Baptists, Presbyterians, and Methodists. The Second Great Awakening reached almost as great a height of religious intensity as had the first, but partly because it affected nearly all the Protestant sects it did not end in the bitter controversies and recriminations that had characterized the final outbursts of the first revival in so many congregations.

One outcome of the first Great Awakening and the years of controversy that followed, as well as of the Revolution and the liberal philosophies of the late eighteenth century, was the gradual breaking away of the nonenthusiasts and the less orthodox Congregationalists. The Unitarians, who did not have even one church until well after 1800, by 1825 had 125 congregations in New England, principally in Massachusetts. This church embraced those Congregationalists who had no sympathy with the soul searchings of the Awakening, rationalists who were secretly or openly in sympathy with the liberalism of the day, and essentially nonreligious Protestants who were unwilling to accept the strict discipline and stricter creed of seventeenth- and eighteenth-century Puritanism. One Episcopal church also went over to Unitarianism.

In the course of the early nineteenth century, then, New England Protestantism by and large took one of two courses:

Interior of the Village Meetinghouse.

either it strengthened its position and increased its membership through revivals or it made concessions to the temper of the time.

The concessions, in whatever sect, sometimes took forms that seem ludicrous to us today. One of them was known as the "stove controversy," and because it revolved about material rather than heavenly comforts it aroused strong feelings wherever it became an issue. Stoves were a late arrival on the New England scene, and they were not generally installed in meetinghouses until after 1820. Before that time members of the congregation had taken foot and hand warmers to meeting or had suffered stoically. Many of the stoics objected to the proposed stoves as alarming innovations, dangerous fire hazards, causes of consumption and other ills of the flesh, and general debauchers of religious fortitude. When the minister of a small town in New Hampshire wanted to install a stove in 1812 one of his parishioners retorted, "If Mr. Merrill needs a fire, let him go to the place where they keep one the year round."

In Simsbury, Connecticut, a committee appointed in 1817 to purchase two iron stoves for the meetinghouse met so much opposition that it finally abandoned the effort, and the stoves, dubbed by scornful parishioners "grand, gloomy, and peculiar," were not installed until after 1821. It took ten years to get a stove into the Rowley, Massachusetts, meetinghouse. In Southington, Connecticut, in 1831, a stove was connected in the meetinghouse basement and services held there for seven years while the congregation debated whether or not to install heat upstairs. In almost every case there was considerable opposition and argument, a pro-stove vs. anti-stove war that seems ridiculous to us today but was deadly serious to the determinedly freezing or would-be-warm congregations of the early nineteenth century.

The singing controversy was another issue. That difficulty had its origins in the eighteenth century, when people with any ear for music became fed up with the cacophonous singing of the congregations. A reform in the direction of part singing, unison singing, and voice training in singing schools did much to ease the strain on aural nerves but caused bitter opposition. Even when a congregation agreed to the new mode, there was endless bickering over who should appoint the choir, who should lead it, where it should sit, how often and where it should practise, and a host of other equally critical decisions. In Abington, Massachusetts, the church and the town appointed separate choirs, and on a Sabbath in February 1806 the rival choirs each broke into a different song at hymn time, causing the congregation to rise in uproar, the minister to carry out his swooning wife in his arms, and one cool head in the congregation, a lawyer, to stand in the aisle and write out a list of the noisy offenders.

By 1800 this battle had been largely won by the choirs, but there remained another issue, that of admitting instrumental music to the meetinghouse. Organs had occasionally appeared in Episcopal churches, but the first in a Congregational meetinghouse, the First Church in Providence, was later removed. As late as 1809 Elias Boudinot came upon only one in his tour of New England. About that time organs began to be introduced, once more first in Providence again, then in Boston, and gradually in the smaller Congregationalist towns. The bass viol, the flute, and the violin were also gradually admitted within the precincts of Congregationalism. In Harvard, Massachusetts, the church voted in 1795 to suspend the playing of the bass viol, recently introduced, but the choir forced a reconsideration two years later. In Braintree, Massachusetts, one member walked out of meeting in 1804 on the day the bass viol was brought in, muttering as he departed that "he did not want to go into God's House to hear a great fiddle." The congregation in Shirley, Massachusetts, more musical perhaps than their contemporaries, approved the purchase of a bass viol in 1787 and even procured a chest to keep it in.

Other minor changes took place in the Puritan churches. Kneeling at prayer, anathema as papal trumpery to seventeenth-century New England, gradually became accepted practise. Annual fasts in each state, formerly strictly observed, gradually became a custom of eating lightly once or twice a day or eating a meal of plain foods. State governors gradually began to change the name from Day of Fast and Humiliation to Day of Prayer. The Reverend William Bentley of Salem, observing this change in 1819, noted that "few fast. Some vary their meals and put off the eating of meat till supper or after the evening service. Most make no other change than to have no parade, perhaps a more simple dinner and without any invitations to their friends, which are not uncommon on Sundays among their more dependant relatives." He noted, too, as early as 1806, that "it is a late thing but quite common, to dedicate meetinghouses. We shall soon steal the name churches as we have gowns and organs." Samuel Goodrich in 1856 noted that the word "church" had been substituted for "meetinghouse" among the Congregationalists only within the preceding ten years.

Sabbath observance itself began to change. The strict Sabbath keeping observed by the French officers stationed in New England during the Revolution began gradually to give way to a more lenient attitude. In 1787 families on Sundays still kept "very close, except when at public worship, . . . and perhaps in the evening at home reading to one another, when not called to family prayers, [and] in singing of Watts' Psalms and Hymns." A few years later the Rev. William Bentley reprimanded one of his flock for riding out on Sunday, and Elias

Boudinot commented that the Sabbath was much more strictly observed in New England than it was in his native New Jersey. Yet the minister of Goshen, Connecticut, commented in 1812 on nonattendance at service and traveling on the Sabbath as "a growing evil," and the newspapers of the day printed letters and editorials deploring the increasing laxity. But as late as the 1840's most New Englanders regularly attended Sunday service, and no railway trains or steamship lines operated on that day.

The real impact of New England Puritanism in the nineteenth century, however, was not so much the emergence of new sects, the relaxing of the ancient discipline, and the strengthening of existing churches through revivals as it was in the channeling of the religious impulse into a humanitarian effort. The same conscience that compelled New Englanders to search deeply into their motives, to acknowledge their sinfulness, and to promise atonement led them, once they began to turn the searching outward, as they did increasingly after the Great Awakening, to pioneer in a host of reform movements. In the 1790's there began among the Connecticut churches a powerful antislavery campaign. Connecticut had already provided for gradual emancipation within its borders, but now the attention of its citizens was directed toward the evils of slavery outside the state. Jonathan Edwards of New Haven, son of the great revivalist preacher, was leader of the Anti-Slavery Society, formed in 1790. In 1817 the African Colonization Society was organized and won fervent support from the New England churches and congregations. The activities of this society channeled directly into the widespread antislavery movement that followed the Missouri Compromise of 1820.

Humanitarianism operated in other directions as well. Interest in prison reform began in New England after 1800. Previous to that time debtors and criminals alike had been herded into dark, unheated, ill-ventilated, unsanitary quarters and left to their own devices. The reform movement worked for separate cells, adequate light and heat, and the reclaiming of prisoners through religious instruction, wholesome labor, and solitary confinement during nonworking hours. Solitary confinement, repugnant to the penological thought of the twentieth century, was at least an improvement on the ancient practice of confining together all classes of criminals and debtors, young and old, in one area.

Hospital building and the care of destitute children, the deaf and dumb, and the insane were other aspects of New England humanitarianism in this period. The first school for the deaf and dumb was founded at Hartford in 1817, as was a hospital for the insane in 1824. Boston opened the first school for the training of the blind. Orphan asylums were started in several communities. These efforts were a far cry from the casual attitude with which unfortunates had formerly been treated, when, following the older English system, children otherwise unprovided for were apprenticed to a trade or a household, the insane were imprisoned, left in the care of relatives, or boarded out, and the physically disabled received no community aid whatever. This was the era too when many towns were setting up poorhouses, thus doing away with the old system of outdoor relief and warning the poor from town to town.

The churches also interested themselves in women's education. A series of female seminaries sprang up in New England, most of them with the aid and approval of local clergymen. They were founded and staffed for the most part by women seriously concerned with educating young girls to assume the responsibilities of adulthood with some awareness of their obligation to God and to society. The seminaries were dubbed "ministers' rib factories," so frequently did their graduates marry into the ranks of the clergy. From these efforts came the nation's first women's colleges.

The missionary movement and interest in charitable aid also grew out of the evangelical impulse. Missionaries sent out by individual churches, by the consociations and synods were supported by the people back home, both financially and by their prayers and good wishes. Women of the different churches worked hard to gather, pack, and send clothing, bedding, and other necessary articles to the western missions, the new churches in Maine and Vermont, and to the missions overseas. Many women organized female cent societies or other organizations to which they contributed regularly for the support of the missions.

Thus by the 1830's New England Protestantism, both Congregationalism and the sects that had broken off from it or organized in opposition to it, was a vigorous element in the lives of New Englanders. The self-contained but militant, learned but intolerant Congregationalism of the seventeenth century, promising as it did glorious salvation to its elect and eternal damnation to all others, had given way first to despair or indifference at the end of that century, then to the enthusiasm and rationalism of the eighteenth century with its sectarian divisions, and finally to the enlightened Protestantism of the early nineteenth, somewhat less soul-searching except in rarer moments of doubt or revival, with its heart and mind beginning to turn outward to the needs of the less enlightened and the unenlightened. The seventeenth-century Puritan somewhere along the line had developed a maternal instinct. His interest in humanitarianism, in the northern, western, and foreign missions, gave him a new orientation, although he was never completely to lose the conscience and the subjectivity that would mark him forever as a Puritan, a New Englander, and sometimes as an American. It was in the early nineteenth century too that New Englanders began migrating in great numbers to the north and west. They settled upper New Hampshire, Vermont, and Maine, and they pushed westward into the Ohio Territory, the Illinois country, and beyond. Wherever they went, they carried with them the conscience, the conviction—or sometimes lack of it—and the attitudes of life that we today call New England Puritanism.

The graveyard.

The Candia Schoolhouse.

The Candia Schoolhouse   4

In the early nineteenth century every New England town had one or more town schoolhouses or district schools. These were elementary schools that taught children to read, write, and do simple sums. They were usually taught by a woman for the ten weeks' summer session, by a man in the three months of winter. Children attended or not at the will of their parents, but the towns had no option. They were required to furnish at least this amount of schooling.

The Candia Schoolhouse, a small building with a rough board exterior, was District Schoolhouse No. 7 in Candia, New Hampshire. It was probably built soon after the War of 1812, certainly prior to the inauguration of John Quincy Adams in 1825. The building was small, mean, poorly insulated, and stood on a triangle of the road, a spot neither quiet nor desirable. For some reason it was not even clapboarded; its lap-jointed, bevel-edged sheathing even today serves as the outer shell. There is a chimney at either end but no evidence of a fireplace. Two windows on each side, the original door in front, and a second door recently cut out at the side to facilitate the flow of visitor traffic provide the only ventilation and light.

In 1953 the Candia Improvement Club, which then owned the building, gave it to Old Sturbridge Village. It was re-erected in the Village in 1961 through the generosity of the club and of the Spaulding-Potter Charitable Trust of Concord, New Hampshire.

Inside the front door of the Candia Schoolhouse is an entry where the children might hang their outer clothing and a wood-box, servant of the ravenous schoolroom stove. The school-room is furnished along three walls with rows of benches with broad tops that serve as desks. The floor slopes to the teacher's tall desk near the door. There are no blackboards, no maps, no pictures, no colorfully illustrated texts—indeed no texts of any kind except at the teacher's desk—no color on the walls. Education in the early nineteenth century was a deadly serious process, liberty in the schoolroom unheard of. The contrast with today's public schools could not be greater. Yet drab and humble as it is, this building represents an ideal held by New Englanders and unknown to any other peoples of the seventeenth and eighteenth centuries: universal literacy.

The first New England education law was passed by the Massachusetts General Court in 1642; by that act selectmen in each town must require parents and guardians to teach their children to read and to understand the laws and religious principles of the colony, and to put them to some useful work. Connecticut enacted a similar law in 1650. In both colonies the intent behind the law was evident. Puritanism required a literate laity, one that could read the Bible, learn the catechism, and understand the way to salvation. Even before the act of 1642, the Massachusetts General Court in 1636 established Harvard College for the express purpose of educating ministers.

The first act relating to school education was passed in Massachusetts in 1647. Every town with a population of fifty families or more was to appoint a schoolmaster to teach the children to read and write, his wages to be paid by the parents and masters. Every town containing a hundred or more families must establish a grammar school to prepare youths for the college.

The New Haven Colony had set up a free school in that town in 1641 and in 1657 required that every plantation in the colony set up a school, which would be supported in part by public funds. After New Haven merged with Connecticut, the United Colony of Connecticut in 1672 granted land to the county towns of Fairfield and New London to support grammar schools and in 1677 imposed a fine on towns neglecting to maintain schools. The schools at New Haven and Hartford, the capital towns, were free Latin schools. County towns neglecting to maintain a Latin or grammar school were required to forfeit an annual fine of ten pounds to the nearest town within that county that kept a Latin school. Plymouth Colony had such a school after 1670. In New Hampshire, Portsmouth opened a grammar school about the year 1696.

It is clear that what is meant in nearly every case is a grammar school, that is, a school where boys were admitted only after they could read English and where the principal subject taught was Latin. The Boston Latin School, still in existence, was begun in 1635 or 1636. Salem started a Latin school in 1637 and in 1677 listed its subjects of instruction as "English, Latin, Greek, good manners, and the principles of the Christian religion"; the aim of the school was to fit its scholars "for the university if desired and they are capable." The Portsmouth Grammar School was to teach its students "tongues and good manners." By 1700 there were thirty-five grammar schools in New England, not one of them in Rhode Island. Most of the Harvard students came from the schools in Boston, Cambridge, Roxbury, and Charlestown, all in Massachusetts.

The grammar schools, however, were limited both in purpose and student body, not really popular with the people, and were not lasting institutions. The lack of enthusiasm with which they were regarded may account for the decline in literacy evident after 1660. In Gloucester in 1664 it was estimated that fully half the population was unable to read or write. Natick, Massachusetts, in 1698 had seventy children of school age but no schoolmaster; only one of these children was able to read.

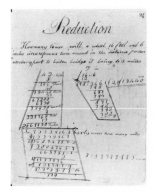

Connecticut Colony, which had never fully approved the grammar school idea, in 1700 enacted a law requiring every town containing seventy or more families to have a full-time instructor to teach children to read and write and towns containing fewer families to employ a teacher for six months of the year. A grammar school was to be maintained in each of the four county towns.

It was clear by the early eighteenth century that more than grammar schools were needed. Some town schools taught reading and writing as well as Latin grammar, but school terms were irregular, children attended only a few weeks in the year, and few got beyond a clumsy ability to read, write, and cipher. Many adults could neither read nor write, and it looked as though the high literacy standards of the early Puritans were gone for good. The Reverend John Danforth in a sermon in 1704 thundered, "hundreds of children in a town, and scandalous neglect of them, perhaps not a tenth of them taught at schools all the year long." Cotton Mather in 1711 complained that "the country is perishing for want of [education]; they are sinking apace into barbarism and all wickedness."

Massachusetts Bay attempted to remedy the evil in 1714, requiring that towns of five hundred families or more were to maintain two grammar and two writing schools. Actually the grammar schools were fast disappearing, and the moving and district school were taking their place if not fulfilling their exact functions.

The eighteenth century saw the development of several different types of schools in New England: the dame school, the moving school, the district school, private schools and academies, and seminaries for young ladies. The district school became the prototype for the primary schools of the mid-nineteenth century, the dame schools for the later kindergartens, and the academies and seminaries for the high schools.

The dame schools go back in origin to the seventeenth century, when boys were admitted to the grammar schools only after they had learned to read and write English and girls were not admitted at all. Some way had to be found to teach small children the alphabet and get them through the hornbook and first reading of the Bible. Parents could teach the little ones at home or send them to private schools. These elementary private schools were known as dame schools because they were kept by some spinster or housewife who was willing to take in the children at a nominal fee, teach them their letters, instruct the little girls in the fundamentals of sewing and knitting, and generally act as a glorified nursemaid. Occasionally these dame schools, as in Dudley and Greenfield, Massachusetts, in 1749, were authorized and supported by the town.

Isaac Parker of Malden, Massachusetts, born in 1776, remembered of the school he attended "that the only book he had was the Psalter. After he had read and spelled a little, he was usually put to shelling beans or some other useful and improving occupation."

William Allen of Industry, Maine, recalled:

An old maiden lady was employed occasionally, a short time, to teach children their letters and to spell out words. Her school was kept one month in my barn. She did what she could to teach the young idea how to shoot, but was quite incompetent. I visited her school on one occasion and she had a small class advanced to words of three syllables in the spelling-book, and when they came to the word "anecdote," she called it "a-neck-dote," and defined it to be "food eaten between meals."

A resident of Dublin, New Hampshire, described the dame school he had attended as,

. . . in an old dilapidated dwelling house, with rough slabs taken from my grandfather's sawmill for seats, and these upheld by sticks driven into large auger holes, with nothing to support the feeble backs of the feeble-minded boys and girls that sat thereon . . . . On one side of the room, thus strangely metamorphosed into a "Temple of Science," were ranged the long dressers, where the good dame of the house, with exquisite taste, had been accustomed to display her pewter platters and wooden plates, her brown earthen mugs and iron spoons; while underneath were the noble cupboards, where time and again she had stored the bean-porridge and hasty pudding—those choice viands of a former generation.

The Beecher children of Litchfield, Connecticut, attended dame school at

Ma'am Kilbourne's, on West Street, and there he [Henry Ward Beecher] clambered up the first rounds of the ladder of book learning and took his first lessons. These consisted in repeating his letters twice a day, such as he could remember, and having the others pointed out to him from Webster's spelling book, as he stood, a chubby barefooted, round, rosy-faced boy, in front of the dreaded schoolma'am, who had been made sharp and angular by her years of labor in shaping the intellectual faculties of generations of children.

The moving school was a step in the development of the district school. It was exactly what its name implies, a school held in different parts of the town, moving periodically from section to section. The logic behind it was that in this way every child would have the same advantage of living near the school for part of the term. Thus was Andover's moving school established in 1729:

Philemon Robbins came first to keep a school in Andover and began his school in the south end of the town and continued there three months, and then went behind the pond in the first day of December and continued there until the last of January, and then was sent and continued in the middle of the town into the last of February next, and then was sent behind the pond in the third day of March, and to continue there fourteen nights, and then the 16th of March was returned to the middle of the town and continued there nine weeks.

The moving school was forced on town meetings by parents living in outlying sections and was a direct result of town taxation for school support. It was a purely New England application of the principle of utilitarianism, and however deplorable its effects it was democracy in action. It grew out of the indifference or hostility to town schools earlier noted by Cotton Mather, and was the principal manifestation of that hostility. As parents became more and more reluctant to pay tuition for their children and as the towns were forced to fall back on taxes, the townspeople began to exercise their right to determine who should pay and how, and how the schools should be conducted. That debate is still going on today. In the eighteenth century, most towns authorized the moving school by popular vote.

The indifference to education, or at least opposition to its expense, continued throughout most of the eighteenth century and reached its peak during the Revolution. Many towns closed their schools for long periods during the war. In Bristol, Rhode Island, there was no school from 1772 to 1781. Manchester and Weare, New Hampshire, closed their schools in 1775, and Swanzey schools were closed in 1775 and 1776. Old Lyme, Connecticut, suspended both its district schools and summer sessions in 1774. The town vote usually was "to drop the schooling for the present." Jeremy Belknap scored his state in his *History of New Hampshire*, for there not only the frontier,

but many other towns, large and opulent, and far removed from any danger by the enemy, were, for a great part of the time, destitute of any public schools; not only without applying to the legislature for permission; but contrary to the express requirements of law, and notwithstanding courts of justice were frequently holden, and grand jurors solemnly sworn and charged to present all breaches of law, and the want of schools in particular. This negligence was one among many evidences of a most unhappy prostration of morals during that period. It afforded a melancholy prospect to the friends of science, and of virtue; and excited some generous and philanthropic persons to devise other methods of education.

In the words of a Connecticut historian, "It was a time of rapid decline in educational advantage with increasing illiteracy among the people."

Where moving schools were not set up the regular English, or writing, schools continued. Lexington built a grammar school in 1714, converted it to a moving school, and after 1760 set up schools to teach small children and those who would not learn Latin. Mendon, Massachusetts, set up a "reading and writing school" in 1721, but with the provision that it should cease if the town were required to maintain a grammar school. Salem, New Hampshire, set up a "riting, sifering, and reding school" in 1759. In 1770 there was a battle in town meeting when a large number of Salem householders refused to assign money to this school. Apparently the school ceased, because in 1775 the town was fined for not complying with the legislative requirement in regard to education. The town meeting refused to reimburse the selectmen who had paid the fine, and it was not until 1778, after the worst struggles of the war were over, that Salem again had a school. Farmington, Maine, opened an English school in 1788 and each student paid tuition. Women taught in this school during the summer.

Northfield, Massachusetts, built a new schoolhouse in 1764, a single room twenty-one by twenty feet, seven feet high, with a chimney at one end and the teacher's desk at the other. At this time the town decided to dispense with individual tuition, though the students' families were required to furnish wood for the fireplace. Ridgefield, Connecticut, which built a new schoolhouse in 1744, voted at a "sheep meeting" two years earlier that "the money coming from the hire of the sheep last year shall be given as a bounty to help maintain the town school forever." This bounty, from the letting out of the 2,000 town sheep, continued until 1760. After 1753 Ridgefield had women teaching its summer sessions.

The district schools grew out of the moving schools and the English writing schools. They were the moving schools made stationary in the various districts or squadrons of the town, and their curriculum was that of the English writing school. Connecticut authorized the system in 1766, just before the Revolution. In 1789, after the war, Massachusetts recognized the

SONG BOOK.   31
ROBIN RED BREAST.

LITTLE Robin Red Breaft,
    Sitting on a Pole,
Niddle, Noddle, went his Head,
    And Poop went his Hole.

PRONTO.

system and legalized it in 1817. Vermont accepted it in 1797, Rhode Island in 1800, New Hampshire in 1805, and Maine in 1817. District schools were the characteristic New England town primary and secondary schools until the mid-nineteenth century. They were largely supported by town tax, supervised by a committee that usually included the ministers and selectmen, and maintained by a prudential committeeman elected by the people of the district.

The least valuable land in the district, usually in the exact center, was considered the best site for the schoolhouse. Often it was on a triangle in the road, exposed to the noise of traffic wheels, the sounds of town activities, the dust and sun of an unshaded spot. Playgrounds were unknown. One clergyman, speaking at the opening of a school in 1839, declared, "Most of the schoolhouses I am acquainted with are about as agreeable to the eye as our pounds, and I fear they are not looked upon by our children with much more pleasure than are those other dull enclosures for our cattle."

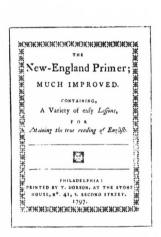

Sarah Bailey describes a district school in Andover, Massachusetts:

The location was usually in the exact territorial centre of the district, however unsuitable the spot might be. The floor of the room sloped up to the back seat; a wood fire blazed at one end of the room; a ferule on the master's desk served the double purpose, to punish idlers and to rap on the window-sash to call scholars into the school. A pile of wood at the door was heaped up for the large boys to saw at odd times. Flagellations were a regular part of the school exercises. The mending of pens also was an important office of the master, who might often be seen with three or four quills stuck behind his ears, and a group of urchins, with inky hands and faces, waiting around, nudging and jostling one another, or watching curiously while the master brought the blunt nib of the pens to a fine point with the sharp knife.

A minister at Brimfield, Massachusetts, wrote caustically to the Massachusetts Historical Society in 1803:

There are ten districts for schools, and nine schoolhouses; but the schoolhouses are mostly out of repair. The one in the middle of the town is small, very inconvenient, and quite old: and although there are nearly one hundred scholars belonging to the district, its inhabitants cannot be convinced at present of the necessity of erecting a new one of a larger and more convenient size.

From the earliest days schools were supported partly by private subscription, partly by rents from lands set aside for schools, partly by tuition fees, and partly by taxes. Most towns supported their schools in more than one way, though usually all required that parents pay some tuition. School support by taxation was not made compulsory in Massachusetts until 1827. Dedham was the first town, in 1649, to have a school supported by general taxation, that is, by a tax on all property holders. Plymouth in 1670 applied rents from its fisheries to school support. In many towns the dog tax went to schools. Newport, Rhode Island, applied the proceeds of a lottery, Springfield the fine on swine roaming at large.

Most towns set apart a certain portion of their lands for the support of ministers and schools. Occasionally an individual left money for school support, as did Comfort Starr of Danbury, Connecticut, in 1763, Captain Ephraim Brigham of Marlboro, Massachusetts, in 1771, Dr. Daniel Lothrop of Norwich, Connecticut, in 1782, and Mrs. Sarah Winslow of Dunstable, Massachusetts, in 1789. Dedham received a large grant in 1812.

Connecticut followed a unique pattern. Here there was an established church, and the church controlled the schools. In 1796 the state appropriated the proceeds from the sale of 3,300,000 acres of its lands in the Ohio Western Reserve to the support of schools, and, under certain conditions, church societies. Church societies acting as school societies were to distribute the funds. The old tax for schools was discontinued in 1821. The net result was that the Connecticut school societies relied on state funds to such an extent that they did not develop adequate financing systems of their own. When costs went up after 1825, they resorted to tuition fees rather than impose local taxes. It was not until 1856 that the State of Connecticut again levied a school tax.

School buildings in the early nineteenth century were one-room, single-story timber houses, usually unpainted. They varied in size but were most often twenty-six by twenty-four feet. The interiors were equally unprepossessing, small, sometimes whitewashed, with high windows from which the glass was often missing, badly lighted, and poorly heated and furnished. The fireplaces and the stoves that later replaced them burned wood supplied by the parents, and this wood ranged from adequate to green, which is totally unfit to burn. Some

The earth is the Lord's and the fulness thereof; the world and they that dwell there in.

19

schoolrooms had single desks and seats, others long desks and benches, others tables where students faced one another. Some schoolhouses were built like amphitheaters, with slanting floors and the teacher's desk in the center well.

Equipment was meager and in some schools furnished entirely by the pupils. When Henry Barnard visited the Connecticut schools in 1837 and 1838 he found only two globes and a few blackboards. Neither piece of equipment was standard until the time of the Civil War. Lead pencils were advertised soon after 1820, but parents had to purchase them. Ink was usually homemade, and until 1850 most children used quill pens. They also had slates and slate pencils. They made their own copybooks at home.

Textbooks were an innovation of the late eighteenth century. Before their introduction learning had been by rote, the dreariest and noisiest method imaginable. The *New England Primer*, first published in the 1680's, had been the first and for long the only text. It was based on the Westminster Assembly's Shorter Catechism and was still being used in dame schools in Boston as late as 1806. Until the publication in 1743 of the *Schoolmaster's Assistant*, written by an Englishman, Nicholas Dilworth, arithmetic was taught without texts. The first modern reader was the *Franklin Primer*, published in 1802, which contained a variety of tables, moral lessons, a concise history of the world, entirely biblical, hymns, and some catechism. Nicholas Pike of Newburyport published an arithmetic in 1788 that became the foremost text of its day. Dilworth published a speller that was pirated in America in 1782, but the most famous speller of all was that of Noah Webster, first published in 1783.

After 1800 the number and variety of texts increased rapidly. There were new arithmetics, spellers, English grammars, geographies by Jedidiah Morse, William C. Woodbridge, Emma Willard, and Samuel Huntington, United States histories, and, later, eclectic readers and books on elocution.

There was no uniformity in the use of texts. Parents expected their children to use anything they happened to have at home. Teachers, school committees, and districts changed texts at will. And there were too few books of any kind. In most districts parents had to furnish them, and when they did not do so the children went without.

The schoolhouse interior.

The school day usually began at nine o'clock and ended at four or five o'clock. School was held five and a half days a week, usually continuing all day Saturday on alternate weeks. The day started with a reading from the Testament, then arithmetic, reading, and spelling in the forenoon. The afternoon repeated the same in somewhat different order. The curriculum was still the three R's, although in 1830 Connecticut added English grammar and geography. The term was generally twelve weeks in winter, ten or twelve in summer.

Teachers varied greatly in quality. At worst they were ignorant, uneducated, uninspired. At best they were well educated, dedicated men and women, sometimes college students teaching for a term or two. Their salaries were appallingly low, and in many communities they were boarded out to the lowest bidders. Not until 1839 were teachers' training schools opened in Massachusetts.

The Candia Schoolhouse is typical of those in New England in its day. All its classes were taught in one room by one teacher, from the smallest pupils just learning their letters to those who hoped to go on to a college preparatory school. No foreign languages were taught, no advanced studies of any kind. The children learned only to read fairly well, cipher, and write a fine hand. Anything more was beyond the province of the district school. Only after 1840 was the high school movement to gain momentum, only then was teacher training seriously undertaken, and only then was serious effort made to see to it that every child attended school and that every town furnished his education free of charge.

Even given its appalling number of children working in the factories, New England was the pioneer in the movement for education freely available to all, and eventually for free education. Henry Ward Beecher's indictment that "the sum of all that we ever got in a district school would not cover the first ten letters of the alphabet" was true but by 1840 it was to be everywhere untrue.

The Law Office 5

Travelers in New England often commented on the region's extraordinary number of lawyers and on their prosperous appearance. There *were* many lawyers, and the reason for their proliferation was probably twofold. Law was one of the two professions (the other being the church) whereby an ambitious young man could aspire to social position. Secondly, New Englanders were an extremely litigious lot, enjoying quarreling with one another over land, livestock, their children's escapades, debts, politics—anything at all—and they frequently felt it necessary to go to law. Most of their causes were minor, requiring the office of the justice of the peace more often than that of the county bench, but they usually necessitated the presence of an attorney.

There were few lawyers in New England before 1750. Lawyers (though not magistrates) were considered not quite respectable in the seventeenth century; in fact it was not until 1708 that the General Court of Connecticut passed its first act admitting attorneys to practise. Twenty-two years later it provided for only eleven lawyers in the entire colony—three in Hartford County, and two in each of the other four. Soon thereafter, however, the legislature had a change of heart: the limitation on numbers was repealed and lawyers were exempted from military duty. By the middle of the eighteenth century they were in New England to stay.

Commercial transactions, settlement of estates, inheritances, land titles, maritime affairs, and admiralty law all demanded the services of men trained in the law. As their numbers and influence grew they began slowly to range themselves as a profession with the clergy. In Massachusetts most were educated at Harvard; in other areas many had studied at the London Inns of Court. By the outbreak of the Revolution, New England had a body of men trained in law, able and ready to play their role in leading the region out of the British Empire.

During the war the lawyers were divided in sentiment. For men trained in the London Inns of Court the dilemma could be heartbreaking. Many members of the Massachusetts Bar remained loyal to the Crown. In Connecticut, on the other hand, no lawyer did so.

When the Revolution was over, those lawyers who had been good patriots and had served their country well suddenly found themselves the objects of suspicion, resentment, and open hostility. Peter the Great, after a visit to the London Courts, had "thanked God that there was but one lawyer in his dominions and declared he would hang him as soon as he got home." The New England farmer fervently echoed the tsar's sentiments. Nor was the dislike limited to farmers; an anonymous pamphlet published in Boston in 1786 declared, "If this order of men are permitted to go on in their career, without some check from the legislature . . . the ruin of the commonwealth is inevitable."

Obviously only a small part of this distrust can be attributed to lawyers' defections to the Crown during the Revolution. Far more important was the fact that most of the legal work of the immediate postwar years concerned the collection of debts and enforcement of contracts. Interruption of business during the war, high prices, and great public debts seriously reduced the fortunes of all classes of people. Loyalists whose estates had been confiscated were making tremendous efforts to have them restored. English creditors were trying to recover their claims. Jails were crowded with debtors. The people as a whole, not just in New England, were irritated by excessive litigation, the increase of suits for debt and mortgage foreclosures, heavy fees and court costs, and they were inclined to blame all their woes on the lawyers.

Interior of the Law Office.

Thus Shays' Rebellion against both the economic situation and the courts and legal profession, which occurred in Massachusetts in 1786, should have been no surprise. A Worcester County convention of 1782 had recommended that lawyers' fees be reduced, that the single probate court in that county be made into four, and that justices of the peace be empowered to decide civil cases up to the value of twenty pounds. In Berkshire County, where creditors were demanding payment at a time when no one had money, court dockets became crowded with creditors' suits. In Worcester such suits more than doubled after 1781; they reached a new peak in Berkshire in 1784. When collections were attempted through court proceedings, the position of the debtor was made worse by the addition of high lawyers' fees and court costs.

Attorneys were among the principal targets of dissatisfaction even before fighting broke out. One Berkshire County farmer called the court of common pleas "a dam'd pack of rascalls." An anonymous Boston pamphlet of 1786, *Observations on the Pernicious Practice of the Law*, asserted:

When a man acts becoming the dignity of the profession [that of the law], he ought to be esteemed by every member in the community. But when any number of men under sanction of this character are endeavouring to perplex and embarrass every judicial proceeding—who are rendering intricate even the most evident principles of law,—who are involving every individual that applies for advice in the most distressing difficulties,—who are practising the greatest art in order to delay every process,—who are studying every method to entrap those who are acting upon the unguarded sentiments of honor and equity,—who are taking the advantage of every accidental circumstance which an unprincipled person might have, by the lenity and indulgence of an honest creditor,—who stand ready to strike up a bargain, (after rendering the property in a precarious state) to throw an honest man out of three quarters of his property—when such men pretend to cloak themselves under the sacredness of law, it is full time the people should inquire "by what authority they do these things."

The Massachusetts rebellion of 1786 had its counterpart elsewhere. In Vermont courthouses were burned. The province of Maine in 1790 attempted to push through the Massachusetts legislature laws forbidding law associations, simplifying legal procedure, and reducing fees. Thus the period 1790–1840 opened not very auspiciously for the legal profession.

The men practising in the New England courts in the early nineteenth century for the most part were men of the middle class, sons of merchants and prosperous farmers whose families were able to give them the necessary education. In comparatively few instances were they sons of professional men, of clergymen, or of members of the bar and bench. They had some money, but they yet lacked position.

Before the Revolution a man could train for the law in two ways: He could offer his services to a practising attorney, pay a fee of a hundred dollars, read law with him, and copy briefs; or he could study at the London Inns of Court, where most Americans studied at the Middle Temple.

No colony officially issued any book of laws except its own statutes. What books were available were studied, as well as some of the law and chancery reports and essays on civil law. Blackstone's *Commentaries* was not published in this country until 1771, although the second American edition was a Worcester imprint.

Before the Revolution, the lawyer's office was his house and he practised part of the time only. During the greater part of the year he farmed or engaged in some other occupation. He took care to attend court when on circuit in his county, listened

attentively, took notes, reported questions of law and practice,
and studied what he had jotted down.

After the Revolution, when suits multiplied and lawyers began to devote more time to their professions, they came to realize that admission requirements should be more stringent. The result, at the close of the eighteenth century, was the formation of county bar associations and the drawing up of strict rules for qualification to membership. The regulations of these associations reveal a marked similarity in their requirements for admission to practice. Meetings of the county bar associations took place twice a year, in March and in September; only those entitled to plead before the state supreme court might attend, and only members in attendance might qualify an applicant as a member of the bar.

In Essex County, Massachusetts, a young man with a college degree might qualify for examination by the bar after studying law for three years, the last two years to have been spent in the office of a practitioner of the supreme court of Massachusetts and the last year in Essex County. A student not a college graduate was required to study in a law office for five years preceding admission. He had to be twenty-one years of age and a citizen of the United States at the time of application for admission to the bar. The fee for his law education was $450 for three years, $150 to be paid at the expiration of each year or for any portion of a year. Students required to study for five years had to pay the same rate each year. Other counties in Massachusetts and in other states had similar requirements.

The alternative to studying in a law office, although not mentioned in the county bar regulations, was attendance at one of the few recognized law schools. William and Mary is usually credited with founding the first American professorship of law, in 1779; at that time only Oxford had such a professorship. In 1790 the College of Philadelphia, later the University of Pennsylvania, appointed James Wilson professor of law. He discontinued his lectures after a few years, and the chair was not again filled for twenty-five years. Columbia appointed James King in 1793. In 1795 he had only two students other than his own clerks and in 1796 none, but he continued two years longer. Transylvania University in Kentucky founded a chair in 1779, and this remained in existence for eighty years.

The private law school, essentially a more specialized and

more elaborate form of law office, originated in New England. In 1784 Tapping Reeve, a Princeton graduate and native of Long Island who had migrated to Connecticut and there qualified for the bar just before the Revolution, opened a law school in Litchfield. He was its sole instructor until 1798, when he was appointed judge of the superior court. He then took as his associate James Gould, later a judge of the supreme court. The school continued under their joint instruction until 1820, when Reeve withdrew. On Gould's retirement in 1833, the school was given up. In the early years of the nineteenth century more than a thousand young men from all over the nation attended this school, among them John C. Calhoun, Marcus Martin, Levi Woodbury, William W. Ellsworth, and Roger Sherman Baldwin. The building was small, only twenty by twenty-two feet. The course of study included attendance at lectures on the law, weekly examination, and reading in the law library. From fourteen to eighteen months were required for completion of the course. Tuition was $100 for the first year, $60 for the balance of the course. Students boarded in private homes in the town, and their social life was made gay indeed by the presence of Miss Sarah Pierce's Female Academy in the same town. The curriculum was comprehensive, intended to cover the whole field of jurisprudence.

Harvard established a professorship of law in 1815, another in 1817, and in 1820 for the first time gave the degree of Bachelor of Laws. Yale founded a chair in the 1820's and in 1843 graduated the first class from its law department. The course at Harvard was a year and a half in length, that at Yale two years.

In every New England state, then, soon after the Revolution the equivalent of a college education plus two or three years' study at law was required for admission to the bar. The New England lawyer, country bumpkin though he might be in other respects, was well educated both in the liberal arts and in his own profession. He could not qualify for examination ignorant of the mysteries of the law. No matter how indifferent, busy, or preoccupied the attorney in whose office he studied, no matter how many tedious hours he was required to spend copying writs, briefs, deeds, and wills, he still had time to devote to reading and studying, and indeed he must do this reading and studying in order to qualify.

The best account we have of student life in a small-town attorney's office is that of John Quincy Adams, who was accepted in 1787 by Theophilus Parsons of Newburyport, then perhaps the most renowned lawyer in Massachusetts. Adams began there early in September, and on his first day

began upon the first volume of Robertson's History of Charles the V which Mr. Parsons recommended as containing an account of the feudal institutions, from which were derived many of the laws which are now established in different parts of Europe. I have already read the book; but thought it would be best to peruse it again. I was no where this day, except at the office and my lodgings.

All that fall Adams continued to read and study, frequently amid repeated interruptions both at the office and his lodgings. He was not devoted to the profession, and he worried considerably about how he would find a place once he was admitted to the bar.

The popular odium which has been excited against the practitioners in this Commonwealth prevails to so great a degree that the most innocent and irreproachable life cannot guard a lawyer against the hatred of his fellow citizens. . . . A thousand lies in addition to those published in the papers have been spread all over the country to prejudice the people against the "order," as it has invidiously been called; and as a free people will not descend to disguise their sentiments, the gentlemen of the profession have been treated with contemptuous neglect and with insulting abuse. Yet notwithstanding all this the profession is increasing rapidly in numbers, and the little business to be done is divided into so many shares that they are in danger of starving one another.

Even by the following summer he still had grave reservations.

I have two long years yet before me, which must be wholly employ'd in study, to qualify myself for anything. I have no fortune to expect from any part, and the profession is so much crowded that I have no prospect of supporting myself by it for several years after I begin. . . . My father says that when he was a student, he heard an old lawyer tell the present Judge Sewall, who was then a student likewise, "that he never knew a lawyer that studied who did not grow rich." The observation made an impression, and his own experience has confirmed it.

Other student journals confirm the experience of John Quincy Adams and reveal much the same sort of training. Hol-

John McClellan, by Jared B. Flagg. (Wadsworth Atheneum, Hartford)

brook Curtis of Watertown, Connecticut, for instance, graduated from Yale, studied in the office of Judge Asa Chapman
of Newtown, and for two years read pretty much the same kinds
of law books studied by Adams.

John McClellan of Woodstock, Connecticut, whose office is
now preserved in the Village, was born in 1767. His father, a
county magnate of some importance, had migrated from Worcester, Massachusetts. He had served his country well in the
Revolution, both in the state assembly in the early years and
as colonel of a regiment. At the end of the war he had been
made brigadier-general in the Connecticut Fifth Brigade of
Militia; he became a successful businessman, a charter member
of the local Masonic Lodge, a proprietor of Woodstock Academy, and was generally prominent in town affairs.

John McClellan prepared for college with two local clergymen, the Reverends Steven Williams and Eliphalet Lyman. He
graduated from Yale College in 1785 and seems to have spent
a happy four years in New Haven. His father reminded him
constantly that he must be prudent and frugal, and as an object
lesson sent him three of his own old shirts to wear to class every
day. When at the beginning of John's last term his father heard
from President Stiles glowing reports of his son's scholarship,

Samuel Huntington, governor of Connecticut, 1786–1796.

he advised the youth to consider carefully whether he wished to take up the scholarly life.

Together with a college classmate, Samuel Huntington, nephew and adopted son of the governor, he took up the study of law in the office of Governor Samuel Huntington of Norwich, a leading jurist. He paid "fifty pounds a year for tuition, board, washing, candles, firewood, library, &c." His routine while studying in Norwich was that of any law student of the day. Soon after breakfast he and his classmate retired to the governor's law office, read law until dinnertime, spent the afternoon in copying writs and letters for the governor, were catechized by him on their reading and on points of law, returned to the house for tea, and then studied again in the office until bedtime. The two young men also attended sessions of the Norwich city court, the New London county court, and the state superior court. John took careful notes of each session. One of the cases of debt involved his father as defendant; the elder McClellan lost the case.

McClellan was not idle. Governor Huntington came frequently into the office to question his two students on their studies, to pose problems, and to explain points of law. John and young Samuel occasionally debated various questions of law with students from other offices. Nor was their social life neglected. They were members of a literary society that debated such questions as "ought the powers of Congress to be enlarged," "is man a free agent," "whether the immortality of the soul can be proved from the light of nature," "is duelling justifiable in civil society." They sleighed. They played the violin, and this practice took much of their leisure time. There were frequent dinner guests and good conversation at the Huntington table. On Sundays they attended meeting and read contemplative works. Evenings there were occasional walks, calls at the homes of friends, invitations to tea, dinners, sleigh rides, and infrequently a ball. The consequence of so social a life, however, was indisposition to work. McClellan writes that after one such strenuous round he "lolled away the afternoon in my great chair in the office, took a nap which recruited my drooping nature so much that I felt vigorous enough to study the evening." The next day John went on a sleigh ride to the town of Scotland. There were occasional musical gatherings and one evening a game called "puzzling board."

McClellan returned to Woodstock when old Governor Huntington became ill. There he entered the office of Charles Church Chandler, succeeding to the practise after Chandler's death. He was admitted to the Windham County Bar in August 1787, just two years after his graduation from Yale.

The John McClellan Law Office, so small it is almost lost among the larger structures along the Green, represents one of the most powerful forces in early nineteenth-century New England, the law. Built in Woodstock in 1796, it was purchased, moved, and re-erected in the Village in 1963–64 through the generosity of one of the Village trustees, George R. Stobbs.

John McClellan erected his office in Woodstock at the same time his father built a house for him. That same year, after having done some traveling in the South and West, he married Faith Williams, only daughter of the Honorable William Williams of Lebanon, one of the Connecticut signers of the Declaration of Independence, and granddaughter of Governor Jonathan Trumbull. The house, a four-square mansion built in 1796, burned down in 1830, but the office was saved to survive into the twentieth century. It is Federal in style, painted white on the exterior and off-white inside. It consists of one room only,

eighteen by fourteen feet. It is heated by a fireplace, contains
shelving and closets, and is obviously a simple working office.
No complete record of the original furnishings remained when
the building was acquired by Old Sturbridge Village, and it has
been refurnished as that of a typical rural attorney of the early
nineteenth century. Some of McClellan's library remained, however, and is part of the library in the restored office. The simple
table, chairs, and bookcase are all that were necessary for one
lawyer and probably one or two students studying with him.
The decanter and glasses indicate that he was, in the early days
at least, no strong temperance advocate, and they were no doubt
concessions to clients.

There were 245 attorneys practising law in Connecticut between 1790 and 1840. So far as is known, and the educational
background on many is incomplete, 172 were graduates of
Yale, four of Harvard, four of Brown, three each of Williams
and Princeton, two each of Dartmouth and Union College, one
of Amherst, and one of Trinity. Two had studied law at Yale,
thirty-five at the Litchfield Law School. All but these seven
whose backgrounds are known had studied in the office of a
practising attorney.

Lists for the other New England states reveal the same pattern of college training or its equivalent plus study in a law
office. There were still left a few jurists of the old school, but
they were fast disappearing. One of them, John Dudley of the
New Hampshire bar, on one occasion after his elevation to the
bench gave the following charge to his jury:

Gentlemen of the jury, the lawyers have talked to you of the law. It is not law
we want, but justice. They would govern us by the common law of England.
Trust me, gentlemen, common sense is a much safer guide for us,—the common
sense of Raymond, Exeter, and the other towns which have sent us here to try
this case between two of our neighbors. It is our business to do justice between
the parties, not by any quirks of the law out of Coke or Blackstone—books
that I never read and never will—but by common sense and common honesty
as between man and men. And now, Mr. Sheriff, take out the jury and you,
Mr. Foreman, do not keep us waiting with idle talk, of which there has been
too much already about matters which have nothing to do with the merits of
the case. Give us an honest verdict, as plain common-sense men, and then you
need not be ashamed.

Theophilus Parsons said of Judge Dudley, "You may laugh at

his law and ridicule his language, but he is, after all, the best judge I ever knew in New Hampshire."

In the library of the Yale Law School are the daybooks and records of Barzillai Slosson, graduate of Yale in the class of 1791, who on graduation went to Sharon, Connecticut, and served as tutor at the academy there while he studied in the office of John Cotton Smith. He was admitted to the Fairfield County Bar in 1793. About a year later he moved to Kent and went into practise for himself. Mabel Seymour, who has studied his papers, records that his daily routine included attending trials, advising clients or assisting other lawyers in advising theirs, investigating shop contracts, drawing leases, deeds, and bonds for deeds, attending arbitrations, examining claims, making out partnership agreements, taking depositions, writing wills, and searching for wills.

Slosson's criminal cases were limited chiefly to petty crimes and misdemeanors—assault and battery, desertion of wife or husband, petty theft, destruction of property, abuse of an apprentice or other minor. Twice a year he attended sessions of the county and superior courts at Litchfield. Court week or court days were observed with great festivity in the county seats, and Litchfield with its beautiful new courthouse was no exception. Everyone from all the surrounding towns who could spare the time attended at least one session of the court. The front seats in the courtroom were occupied by gentlemen of some social standing; farmers and common folk crowded into the back. The young men of Tapping Reeve's School and other law students sat in the gallery. Teamsters stopping by, storekeepers, innkeepers, free Negroes, artisans, and apprentices all stole time to watch.

Barzillai Slosson, like his colleagues, occasionally took in law students. He was paid $40 a year. He seems to have had at least seven students between 1801 and 1813. One of his ledgers contains a list of the books in his library in 1806, presumably used by the students in his office as well. He owned about 110 books, sixty-four of which were law books. They included most of the usual titles: Coke, Powell, Blackstone, Bacon, Morgan, Buller, Swift, Espinasse, Root, and Grotius.

John McClellan had no easy time of it at first, in spite of the

fact that he began in his native town and succeeded to another's
practise. Several times he considered moving to Pennsylvania,
Ohio, or Georgia. In 1808, mulling over Ohio, where young
Huntington was already in residence, he complained:

From the state of things here, it is next to an impossibility to collect any money.
Scarcely any of the produce of the country has been sold, and there is no money
or any way that one can commence. . . . Indeed it has been the case that many
men here who were the most punctual have this winter been sued, their property
parted [?] in even though no money will be collected, for there is nobody that
has money to bid off their property. To have therefore put any demands in
writ would have been conceived to no good purpose.

This was written during the darkest days of the Embargo that
preceded the War of 1812, a desperate time indeed for New
Englanders.

The McClellan papers at the Connecticut Historical Society
indicate that he practised regularly at the March, August, and
December sessions of the Windham county court and at the
January and September sessions of the superior court. After
1818 he occasionally appeared at the October session of the
supreme court of errors. Sometimes he attended court in Tolland and Hartford Counties. During a large part of his active
career he also attended the May session of the state assembly
in Hartford and the October session in New Haven.

The remains of his law library, now in his office at Old Sturbridge Village, consist of fifty-odd titles, more than likely only
about half his original library. His accounts and correspondence
show that he added to it steadily and conscientiously, usually
picking up new volumes when attending the legislative sessions
in Hartford and New Haven. He occasionally varied his erudite
fare with a book of poetry or travel. He was one of the earliest
subscribers to the *New England Historical and Genealogical
Register*.

John McClellan's cases varied. For three years, between 1787
and 1790, he handled a probate case, that of one Isaac Winslow, whose estate had been confiscated during the Revolution.
Most of his cases involved debts. Occasionally they were spiced
by quarrels between two towns over responsibility for the support of paupers, controversies involving trespass by reason of
overflow of water, libel, divorce, purchase of a stolen horse,

disagreement over painting a meetinghouse, assault and battery, support of a former slave, overpricing, horse stealing, recovery of an estate, trespass involved in the erection of a mill dam, breach of promise, and failure to contribute to the support of the ministry.

A case that McClellan handled in 1826, dealing with assault, battery, and false imprisonment, had its ridiculous side. The plaintiff, a member of the local militia, had always appeared on training day in uniform. When on one occasion his captain failed to record him as uniformed, the plaintiff determined to have his revenge and appeared at the next training "dressed very shabbily and ludicrously dressed and accompanied by two others similarly dressed. . . . Plaintiff's witnesses swore that his dress was that which he ordinarily wore when he went from home and was better than his everyday dress." The captain thereupon pulled him out of line, held him in custody all day while exposing him to ridicule, and that night fined him and took out a warrant for his arrest and imprisonment.

There are some indications in the McClellan papers of the trials and travails of attending court. When the Windham county courts were sitting in Brooklyn, McClellan boarded with John Parrish, Esq. A doleful letter from Parrish in 1822 revealed that members of the bench occasionally exercised undue precedence over those of the bar: "I had observed that the manner in which Judge Bolles assumed the right of commanding us to leave the parlour was as disagreeable to you as to myself. In order to remedy that evil I have set a Franklin's stove in my northeast chamber, it being the largest room in the house, where I am determined the judge shall sleep and consult their causes, and no more assume the command of the parlour." In one of the places where McClellan occasionally boarded, at Sheriff Williams', "you were sure to find an Indian pudding and a piece of swine's flesh boiled in a pot."

To relieve the tedium, bench and bar regularly got together during the evenings of the court term. One of McClellan's bills, unfortunately undated, was his drinking bill at Windham county court: "three mugs of punch, one bottle spirits, one bottle of brandy, seven bottles spruce beer." His innkeeper's bill for an 1810 session covered "four dinners and club, two breakfasts, four suppers, lemonade and gin, four lodgings, one horse for two nights." Although he owned a chaise, he always

traveled to and from court, in the course of his practise, and to
and from the state assembly, on horseback. The judges arrived
in their own conveyances or by stage.

A bill found in the records of the superior court held in Litchfield in 1808 lists 123 dinners for the judges, seventeen bottles
of Madeira, brandy and sugar, pipes and tobacco, paper and
quills. Salaries may have been low, but there were compensa-
tions.

As late as 1849, just before he suffered the stroke that in-
valided him, McClellan still attended court, though he then
had little business there. He had appeared in court when "older
than any gentleman that ever appeared at the bar as advocate
in Windham County." He had retired officially at the age of
seventy, but could not bear to give up his practise. An old
friend and former student in his office, Samuel Pettes, wrote
that he thought often

of that excellent lot of men which I left in the practice of the law in Windham
County, when I left it for Weathersfield. I have never known such an one since.
Owing to the difficulty of moving from place to place, they were in the habit of
being together for eight or ten weeks every year, and they appeared and acted
like a band of brothers; there was none of that stately distance, which I found
in Hartford County, and which is now found everywhere. Two men can rarely
be found now, who are willing to sleep in the same room, much less in the same
bed.

There are other records of court days. John Quincy Adams
found them a gala period in Newburyport. In Paris Hill, Maine,
a fifer and drummer escorted the justices from the tavern where
they lodged to the courthouse. In York, Maine, where accommodations were poor, the justices and lawyers often had
to share beds as well as rooms. In the evening, when the bar
association met, there were frequent mock courts. One of these
was held at York after a justice absentmindedly left his horse
tied up all night outside a tavern where he had not been able
to secure accommodations. The innkeeper was fined a bowl of
good punch for neglect of an inadvertent guest, the justice
twice that amount for forgetting the animal all night. "The
sentence was carried into immediate execution."

Christopher Columbus Baldwin, who practised in Worcester
County in the 1820's and 1830's, always enjoyed court week.
He recorded a splendid supper attended by justices, attorneys,

and students at law "at which upwards of 70 lawyers sit down and partake. The members of the Court attend and drink many toasts which are remarkable for wit and sense. All insensibly, court & bar, grow quite smutty; tell many lewd stories. . . . None of the company get drunk that I see—leave the table at one A.M." He also noted what appears unique in the annals of New England courts: "According to immemorial use the members of the Bar in Worcester devote the afternoon [after the rising of the court] to rolling nine pins."

Some idea of the increase in lawyers in the early nineteenth century may be gained from a perusal of the Maine records. In 1790 there were sixteen lawyers in the district; in 1800, fifty-four; in 1820, 207; in 1840, 437. New Hampshire had 106 practitioners in 1805. The Duc de la Rochefoucault-Liancourt remarked in 1796 that "the lawyers of Massachusetts have greater influence than any other body of men in the public opinion." Certainly one reason for the enormous increase in the legal profession was the growth of litigation and legal business of every kind.

John McClellan, as did other lawyers in other states, practised in the justice courts, the county courts, the superior court, and the state supreme court. The lowest court of all was that of the justice of the peace. In this court cases were normally limited to settlements of not more than seven dollars, occasionally forty-two dollars, and no appeal could be made if the amount was less than seven dollars. Criminal jurisdiction, in Connecticut at least, was fixed at a maximum fine of seven dollars. There was always a right of appeal, except for a conviction for profane swearing, cursing, or Sabbath breaking.

McClellan was a justice of the peace in Woodstock during most of his career. He gave up the post at the age of seventy only because the law required it. Among his papers is a series of attachment writs signed by him as justice of the peace. These involved suits for collection of debts, for support of a fatherless child, for redress against alienation of a woman's affections, for damages in case of trespass, cruelty, and assault and battery. He administered the Freeman's Oath to prospective citizens and voters, forwarded motions to the county seat, and heard minor civil and criminal cases. Occasionally he was asked to give a character reference or to vouch for individuals as qualified for state and federal appointments. John Adams once sourly remarked of the office of justice of the peace that it "is a great acquisition in the country and such a distinction to a man among his neighbors as is enough to purchase and corrupt almost any man."

Most country lawyers gained only part of their income from legal practise. Many farmed, at least on a part-time basis. Others had business interests in their communities or supplemented their incomes with the fees they took in as justice of the peace or county surveyor or from some other office. Many entered politics and served in the state legislature, where their acquaintance with the great and the near great gave them an entrée to prospective clients. Frances Wright when she visited this country in 1819 was told that young men often trained as lawyers "because if they discover talents and ambition it is considered the best introduction to political life."

Along with holding the office of justice of the peace for Woodstock for forty-five years, John McClellan was a member of the Connecticut state assembly, a national elector for a score of years, a notary public, an occasional agent for manufacturers and other business interests, and a businessman himself. He was a member of a company organized to build a canal from Norwich to the Massachusetts line, of a group interested in establishing a new stage line, and of the Arnold (cotton) Manufacturing Company in Woodstock. For some years he was in partnership with his brother in a retail merchandising operation.

He was at least a part-time farmer, and a large portion of his income seems to have come from this pursuit. While his children were young he engaged a tenant farmer, later farmed with his sons. His principal crops were potatoes, corn, and pumpkins, although his apples were highly thought of, his beef prized, and his butter famous for its quality as far away as Providence.

While most country lawyers built offices near their homes or on the main street of the village, as did John McClellan, other offices might be set up in a room in the lawyer's residence, in a commercial building, or even in a courthouse. One office in Maine was in the second story of an old building built before the Revolution. "The rest of the upper stories were used for dwellings, and the lower portion for pigs and wood, the boards and clapboards of this portion having been taken off and used for firewood. You would not expect a learned lawyer in full robes from such a receptacle." Another office in the same state, described by its occupant, was in a tavern chamber "in which were then arranged three beds and half a table and one chair. My clients had the privilege of sitting on some of the beds. In this room I slept, as did also sundry travelers frequently, the house being a tavern."

In 1831 Christopher Columbus Baldwin saw in Walpole, Massachusetts, an office "which had been sadly mangled and mutilated by having a cannon, charged with brickbats, chain links, broken iron and earthen [sic] fired through it. It was placed before the door and a slow match set off, sending its miscellaneous contents completely through the tenement. The Lawyer had done something that gave offense to a couple of miscreants who took this course to revenge their injury."

Baldwin also noted the astonishing story of Eliakin Davis of Fitchburg, who in 1830 actually brought about the arrest of the high sheriff of Worcester County on some trivial charge.

Perhaps no man ever lived who had manifested throughout so great a fondness for contention. He has been imprisoned again & again for perjury, maintenance and defaming the names of honest citizens, and yet no sooner is he set at liberty than he gets into some scrape for which he is severely punished. He has squandered a good estate in quarrelling with his neighbors and, notwithstanding his poverty, still succeeds in getting funds to carry on his suits. He left Rutland in 1820, or thereabouts, and moved to Fitchburg, where he married a respectable widow lady, with a small real estate, and, from his litigious temper, has become a terror to all the people of the town. His love of the law seems to have become a passion, and every other feeling is made subservient to it. I do not think he would steal or cheat, and I believe he is temperate in his habits. A perfect history of him may be found on the records of Court for the County of Worcester, where he has regularly appeared at every term for near or quite thirty years. In all civil suits he appears as plaintiff, but in criminal matters he is generally on the defensive. He always has about a dozen suits that are to be brought, and if any attorney consents to say anything to him beyond asking after his health, he will give an exact detail of all his cases and, perhaps, produce his papers, all of which must be read, and then comes a request to engage as his counsel; and if he cannot persuade you to it peacefully, he will resort to threats and tender money for a writ or warrant.

Here indeed was one of the New Englanders who was con-

stantly at law and who caused the multiplicity of lawyers.
Thus the "mob of advocates" observed by the Duc de la
Rochefoucault-Liancourt in Connecticut existed because of a
contentious populace, clamoring for legal services.

John McClellan practised law until he was in his eightieth
year and retired then only because he was felled by a stroke.
By that time, the late 1840's, the practise of law had greatly
changed. The cases of trespass, land title, debt, and foreclosure
began to make way for cases involving water rights, turnpike
tolls, articles of association, and the like soon after 1800, and
these cases along with others of their kind increased after the
War of 1812. The rise of both small enterprises and large-scale
industries, the development of roads, canals, and railroads, insurance companies and banks, the increased tempo and en-
largement of commercial transactions—all meant changes and
developments in the law and a different practise on the part
of the lawyers. Less frequently were they appearing in the
justice court in cases of assault and battery or small claims;
more frequently were they counsellors for banks, industries,
commercial firms, and insurance companies. Corporation and
patent law, unknown in the colonies, became increasingly important branches, and lawyers skilled in these seldom needed
to enter the courtroom. Specialization was to take over the
legal profession as it did many another, and the break with
English law would be almost complete by the outbreak of
the Civil War.

The Village Tavern.

The Tavern

6

Late in life John Adams declared that it was from listening to townsmen's discussions at evening tavern gatherings when he was on the judicial circuit that he had come to realize American independence was both inevitable and close at hand. Through a century and more the New England taverns had been breeding grounds for revolution.

The governing bodies of both towns and colonies recognized that commerce and industry were possible only if there were good communications and that good communications could be achieved only through decent roads and accommodations for travelers. Perhaps even more important in the early years was the necessity for a place where members of the congregation might thaw out and refresh themselves in winter between the morning and afternoon Sabbath services held in an unheated meetinghouse.

These needs led Connecticut in 1644 to require each town to provide an inn or ordinary with an innkeeper, licensed by a magistrate, for the "entertainment [of] strangers and passengers." To curb the local trade, townspeople were forbidden to loiter more than half an hour in drinking, and keepers of ordinaries were forbidden to allow anyone to drink more than a third of a pint of sack (sherry). They were not allowed to sell to minors or apprentices except by the written permission of the parent or master, and even then under strict conditions:

"nor at any time except in case of necessity, and then in moderation." Indians were to be served only what they could drink in the innkeeper's presence. Later the town selectmen were to nominate men they thought suitable to keep houses of entertainment, who then had to be licensed by the county court.

In 1660 Massachusetts passed essentially the same legislation. Tavern keepers there must erect "some inoffensive sign . . . for the direction of strangers," must provide stables for horses, and, if their houses were a mile or less from the meetinghouse, must clear them on lecture day of all able to attend the services. In New Hampshire licenses might be granted only to those of good repute who had a good house "and at least two beds to entertain strangers and travellers."

Out of these regulations grew the taverns of the eighteenth century, noisy, crowded, frowned on by the clergy—the clubs of the Radicals and the political schoolrooms of the yeomanry. More often than not they were single dwellings in which the upper chambers had been given over to lodgings, a barroom installed on the main floor, dining area provided in a parlor or in the family living quarters, and a stable built on.

A new age in travel set in after the Revolution. The era of turnpike roads, of stagelines, of wagon trains of supplies for the larger towns and ports, and of drovers with their herds of cattle meant that towns along the routes had more travelers than ever before to provide for. Not only was there greater traffic, with consequently higher maintenance costs and greater demand for state or privately subsidized highways, but the communities were forced to license more innkeepers, which they often found distasteful. Expanding markets, commercial activity, and industrial development brought with them an increase in houses of entertainment with bars accessible to townspeople as well as strangers and with a consequent ever increasing problem of drinking. When to this situation a large immigrant population was added after 1835, the answer was a widespread temperance movement, which was to play a part in the decline of the tavern as a social institution.

As early as the 1750's John Adams, then a struggling young attorney, condemned the evils of taverns, and he was to see more of this when he began making the circuit of the Massachusetts and Maine courts. He distinguished, as evidently did few of the inns themselves, between taverns that existed solely for the accommodation of strangers and the retail houses or grog shops, which supplied the "neighborhood necessary liquors." But in both were "the eternal hosts of loose, disorderly people . . . which renders them offensive and unfit for the entertainment of a traveler of the least delicacy." Poverty and need had become determinants in selecting inn and retail shopkeepers.

The consequences of these abuses are obvious. Young people are tempted to waste their Time and Money, and to acquire habits of Intemperance and Idleness that we often see reduce many of them to Beggary, and Vice, and lead some of them at last to Prisons and the Gallows. The Reputation of our Country is ruined among Strangers who are apt to infer the Character of a Place from that of the Taverns and the People they see there. But the worst Effect of all, and which ought to make every Man who has the least sense of his Priviledges tremble, these Houses are become in many Places the Nurseries of our Legislators;—An Artful Man, who has neither sense nor sentiment may be gaining a little sway among the Rabble of a Town, multiply Taverns and Dram Shops and thereby secure the Votes of Taverner and Retailer and of all, and the Miltiplication [sic] of Taverns will make many who may be induced by Phlip and Rum to Vote for any Man whatever.

In 1761 Adams tried to get the Braintree town meeting to reduce its number of licensed houses, and with some success; the town voted to restrict the number of houses to one in each precinct. But evidently the measure was ineffectual; looking back on it years later Adams asserted that "you may as well preach to the Indians against rum as to our people. . . . If the ancients drank wine as our people drink rum and cider, it is no wonder we read of so many possessed with devils." Others of his day, clergy and laymen alike, protested the role played by towns in increasing the drinking habit among the yeomanry, but to no avail.

The taverns of the early nineteenth century were usually ordinary houses converted into inns. Often they were four-square frame buildings with rooms on two floors on either side of a central chimney. Essential were two rooms, a bar and a sleeping chamber, as well as stables. Accommodations might be poor indeed. When General Washington toured New England in 1789 he found the boiled dinner at a Milford, Connecticut, tavern too poor to eat, asked for bread and milk, and was served it with a broken pewter spoon.

The older taverns were usually in the center of the town

near the meetinghouse. At least one worthy was licensed "to keep a house of common entertainment, provided he keeps it near the new meetinghouse." Timothy Dwight, then president of Yale, believed that these "old-fashioned inns were superior to any of the modern ones which I have seen; the food was always of the best quality, the house and all its appendages were in the highest degree clean and neat, the cooking was remarkably good, and the stable was not less hospitable."

When the Marquis de Chastellux stopped at a Massachusetts tavern in 1781, he dried himself "by a good fire, in a very handsome apartment, adorned with good prints, and handsome mahogany furniture." The comfort of the house reconciled his party to the bad weather outside. In Sheffield he much admired the daughter of the house. In his chamber there he found

some books scattered on the tables. The first I opened was the Abridgement of Newton's Philosophy; this discovery induced me to put some questions to my landlord on physics and geometry, with which I found him well acquainted, and that he was besides very modest, and very good company. He is a surveyor, a very active employment in a country where there is perpetually land to measure and boundaries to fix.

The Tavern office.

In Warren, New Hampshire, there were five taverns about the year 1790. They are described in a town history:

These taverns flourished wonderfully and the proprietors all arrived at considerable wealth. The landlords had comely daughters for waiting maids; strong armed sons to attend the great ox teams that stopped to bait or rest over night, or to groom the saddle horses of gentlemen who patronized them. Then the barroom . . . with its great wood fire and loggerhead at white heat, was an excellent loafing place for the nearest neighbors. They assembled here to learn the news from travelers, hear the gossip of the country round and discuss politics. . . . These inns of those old days were good ones, the table was always well set, the cream the sweetest and richest, the butter and eggs always fresh, vegetables and everything else nice, clean white beds, snowy linen sheets, well swept floors, all was light and neat as strong hands could make it.

An Englishwoman, Harriet Martineau, commented on the number of taverns that had scenic wallpapers in their parlors. "It seems to be an irrisistable [sic] temptation to idle visitors . . . to put speeches into the mouths of the painted personages [in these scenes]; and such hangings are usually seen defaced with scribblings. The effect is odd, in wild places, of seeing American witticisms put into the mouths of Neapolitan fisher-

The ladies' parlor.

men, ancient English ladies of quality, or of tritons and dry-ads."

The most important tavern in Ryefield, Massachusetts, was opposite the meetinghouse. Here balls and social gatherings were held; here the stage to Boston stopped twice a week to water both horses and passengers. "The main building was square, with a broad hall running through it, and two rooms on each side. It was two stories high besides the gambrel roof, and there was a long addition in the rear."

When William Ward Thackara of Philadelphia visited New England with his wife in 1820 they found in Tisbury, Massachusetts, accommodations that, though spartan, were at least tranquil after days spent at sea. The sole furniture of their chamber consisted of a low post bedstead, bedding, and wooden chair, but "the bed was tolerable and the linen *clean*, a most excellent quality." In Boston, as one might expect, they fared better, having a large, cool, carpeted chamber, neatly and comfortably furnished, the use of an elegantly furnished up-stairs parlor, and a table to themselves at mealtime.

Poorer travelers and those who arrived when the inn was already crowded would sleep on the floor of the bar or public room. According to one historian of Sturbridge, sleepers there slept around the fireplace "in a circle, their feet to the fire and their heads resting on buffalo robes." The drovers who stopped at New Hampshire taverns carried

their own supplies, even hay and oats for their horses and cattle, but the etiquette of the road required that they should do something for the house by a liberal patronage of the bar. . . . In cold weather they resorted in full force to the barroom where they regaled themselves before the great fireplace on homemade doughnuts and johnnycake; after which, with flip aplenty, the fun grew fast and furious until a late hour, when the landlord banked the fire, and all but the well-to-do-guests who were favored with rooms fell asleep with no other couch or covering than the barroom floor and a blanket brought from home.

Families traveling together and women alone fared some-what better, although it was common practise for two men who were strangers to each other to be asked to share a bed. Families shared a room, while a woman by herself was usually jealously protected by the mistress of the inn. Cleanliness of chamber and toilet facilities varied from place to place. Chronic

complainers usually found both bad. Most travelers found
them adequate for the day.

Mrs. Basil Hall, who traveled in New England in 1827–28, noted that there were two prints that seemed universally to hang in every inn "great and small. . . . the one is General Washington holding in one hand a roll of paper and in the other extended in the position which indicates what the Americans would call a very lengthy speech, at least, that is my feeling of the matter, but perhaps this arises of my being thoroughly sickened of the eternal picture; the other . . . is General Lafayette in a brown wig and greatcoat, looking like a farmer on a cold day."

When the Groton, Massachusetts, tavern opened soon after the Revolution it was a temperance house, "much to the disgust" of most travelers. The three sisters who later ran it installed bunks in the great room for teamsters and drovers and required them to don a pair of sheepskin slippers when they entered. The hall of this inn was papered with the scenic paper commented on by Harriet Martineau.

The barroom or taproom or great room in many taverns had a sanded floor, straight wooden chairs or Windsor chairs, a tall desk where travelers might write, simple tables, and a bar with grate or gate that could be closed during off hours. The bars themselves had glass and pewter mugs, glass beakers and vessels of various sizes, stone and pottery jugs, punch bowls usually of chinaware, mortar and pestle, lemon squeezer, funnels, knives and spoons, and sometimes a bottle or two. A wooden bowl and spoon might be used for mixing. The toddy iron would be kept at the fireplace. Alice Morse Earle, the antiquarian, tells us that the barroom occasionally was hung with bad verse:

"I've trusted much to my sorrow; Buy today. I'll trust tomorrow."

"My liquor's good, my measure just, But, honest Sirs, I will not trust."

"Care killed this Cat. Trust kills the landlord."

"If trust I must, my ale will pale."

The food served could be good, bad, or indifferent, depending on the competency or care of the landlord, the rank of the guest, and the courtesy and appreciation he expressed. One cannot read old diaries and journals without getting the distinct impression that the independence of New Englanders was present in abundant measure in the tavern keepers. When approached politely, or even curtly by other New Englanders, their service was apt to be good. A demanding, supercilious, critical traveler, especially a "foreigner" (who was anyone from outside the region), was likely to get poor accommodations, badly prepared food, and little attention or service. Thus the taverns were good, fair, or downright bad, depending on who you were and your general approach.

In 1704, Madam Sarah Knight, a New Englander who lived all her married life outside the region, stopped at a tavern in Rhode Island.

Here, having called for something to eat, the woman brought in a twisted thing like a cable, but something whiter, and laying it on the board, tugged for life to bring it into a capacity to spread, which having with great pains accomplished, she served in a dish of pork and cabbage, I suppose the remains of dinner. The sauce was of a deep purple, which I thought was boiled in her dye kettle; the bread was Indian, and everything on the table service agreeable to these. I, being hungry, got a little down, but my stomach was soon cloyed, and what cabbage I swallowed served me for a cudd the whole day after.

A famous traveler of the 1740's, Dr. Alexander Hamilton (no relation to the later statesman), found little good liquor in New England taverns. His comment was, "A man's horses are better provided for than himself, but he pays dear for it."

After the Revolution things seem to have been a little better, perhaps as a result of French visitors who had commented freely on the peculiarities of New England taverns and their keepers. When the Marquis de Chastellux stopped at Chandler's Tavern in Woodstock, Connecticut, he was badly received by an old servant maid. "She would make no preparation of even killing a few chickens, before she received the orders of her mistress. Fortunately, however, the latter arrived in a quarter of an hour, in a sort of single horse chaise, and we found her very polite and obliging, she gave us a tolerable supper, and [we] were neatly lodged."

Henry Wansey, an English textile manufacturer, was in New England in the early 1790's. In New Haven "we dined at a very good tavern there. We had on our table mutton, veal, plenty of garden stuff, with cucumbers, a good salad, with cider and brandy, for all of which we paid only a half a dollar, or two and three pence sterling." In Durham, however, only a few miles to the east, he breakfasted at "a very mean house . . . the worst I have seen, the accommodations equally bad, and for which, as is generally the consequence, we paid very dear. Our bread was cake made of rye, and only half baked; beefsteaks fried in lard; veal cutlets very greasy and black; the tea and coffee smoky. Our sugar was from the maple tree."

New Englanders, on the other hand, did much better when they traveled about their own region. The Reverend Ebenezer

Small dining room at the Tavern.

Parkman "found in a tavern near Westboro a haddock dinner which he pronounced very good." In Boston he was served "an excellent dinner of roast turkey." In Marlboro he dined upon roast goose, roast pea-hens, baked stuffed venison, beef, and pork. The Reverend Stephen Peabody of Atkinson, New Hampshire, while on the road frequently "dined upon salmon." Perhaps clergymen were treated especially well.

John Adams liked good food and knew how to procure it, at least in his own region. In 1771 he arrived in Windsor, Connecticut, on his way home from New York, "just as they had got their Indian pudding and their pork and greens upon the table, one quarter after twelve." A few years later, at one Brewster's, he was served "a decent grace before and after meat—fine pork and beef and cabbage and turnip." Just over the Massachusetts line from New York, he was served "a feast —salt pork and cabbage, roast beef and potatoes, and a noble suet pudding, grog and a glass of port." When he was lucky enough to be invited to a private house he was often served "salted beef and shell beans with a whortleberry pudding and cider."

Francis J. Grund, who was in the United States in the 1830's, commented on what he called the "stereotyped" bills of fare in the taverns and public houses. "As far as my experience goes, they all run thus: roast beef, roast mutton, roast lamb, roast veal, roast pork, roast pig, roast turkey, roast goose, roast chicken, roast pigeons, roast ducks, &c. To which, merely by way of appendix, are added the comparatively insignificant items of pudding, pastry, and dessert."

Zadoc Long traveled in Vermont and Massachusetts in the early 1830's. In Waterford, Vermont, he found a tavern "where the keepers did not seem above their business. The ladies, especially, were very polite. They gave us some fine trouts, well-cooked, with various other delicious articles for supper and breakfast—a clean tablecloth, and clean, well-aired beds." In Weymouth he fared less well.

Left this tavern before breakfast, the most miserable entertainment, by the way, that I have ever found. . . . We called for supper—she seemed reluctant to do anything about it—we were finally furnished with a homely slice of fresh beef that had been laid on a hot gridiron, but in no manner cooked & left for us to butter & salt to suit ourselves, a cup of tea & a few dry crackers. Our sleeping

room was shamefully lacking necessary furniture, & for want of proper airing
was so suffocating that, tho' it was a very cool night, we were obliged to sleep
with open windows.

At Plymouth, Massachusetts, he breakfasted "on baker's bread & herrings, an old fashioned Plymouth morning meal."

Harriet Martineau traveled through the White Mountains in the year 1836. At one tavern she "dined well on mutton, eggs, and whortleberries with milk. Tea was prepared at dinner as regularly as bread throughout this excursion." At another inn, the Lafayette Hotel, she was served a dinner of "hot bread and butter, broiled ham, custards, and good tea."

Often travelers on the road were forced to stop at private homes, either because there was no tavern near, because their horses or conveyances had broken down at an inconvenient point, or because the taverns were already filled. Often they fared better than they would have at a tavern, occasionally worse. Lucy Larcom, the American author and educator, remarked that her town of Beverly, Massachusetts, was called Beantown, by townspeople and travelers alike, simply because it adhered to the old custom of baking beans on Saturday evening and serving them on Sunday. "After a while, as families left off heating their ovens, the beanpots were taken by the village baker on Saturday afternoon, who returned them to each house early on Sunday morning, with a pan of brownbread that went with them."

Joseph Plumb Martin, a soldier in the Continental Army, dropped into a New England farmer's home in 1777.

While I was in this house I went into the kitchen where I saw a simple incident which excited my risibility, mauger my fatigue. There was a large pot hanging over a considerable fire, but more smoke. The pot contained, to appearance, a large hock of fresh beef; the water in the pot had ebbed considerably and the meat made its appearance someway above it. Above the top of the meat, surrounded by fire and smoke, sat the old house cat weaving her head one way and the other, and twisting the beef into her face as fast as possible, winking and blinking in the steam and smoke like a toad in a shower. I left her at her occupation and went out.

Cider seems to have been the universal drink in New England homes, and very often at the taverns as well. Thus when in Philadelphia in 1777 John Adams wrote his wife that he missed cider more than anything. "I would give three guineas for a barrel of your cider, not one drop is to be had here for gold."

Accommodations other than food were generally pretty fair in New England, although circumstances sometimes made them less than desirable. John Adams, who was somewhat prejudiced on the subject, thought that in the country houses that sold drinks to townsmen there was "dirt enough, very miserable accommodation of provision and lodging for yourself and your horse." Elias Boudinot, who was turned away from six taverns in New Haven because they were crowded with visitors come to attend a militia review the next day, finally found an "inferior tavern in the skirt of the town," but was here pleasantly surprised to find "very good quarters . . . kindness and attention . . . good beds and everything clean and neat."

When the Reverend William Bentley stopped at Hitchcock's Tavern in Brookfield, Massachusetts, he was disturbed first by the carousing of the townspeople, who did not leave until midnight, and then by the din of the stages starting up and passing in both directions "so that the motion was incessant through the whole night." William Ward Thackara's lodging in Tisbury had a "tolerable" bed "and the linen clean, a most excellent quality."

Christopher Columbus Baldwin stopped in 1833 at a tavern in Montague, Massachusetts, in the Berkshires:

. . . we alighted and examined the premises to see that our quality should not suffer by having slept at a vulgar house. Newcomb . . . catechised the landlady as to her beds, whether the sheets had been changed, what she could give us for supper, and from the resolute manner of his examination, one would have supposed him an officer of the police in pursuit of stolen property. . . . The only part I performed in this comedy was to ask the landlady to let me see her cook our beefsteak which we had bespoken. This she complied with, not, however, without letting me understand that she thought me an indifferent cook.

What of the men and women who kept these taverns? More than one traveler remarked that most tavern keepers seemed to have held the rank of captain in the Revolution, but this seems more often than not to have been a courtesy title only. The innkeepers, like their inns, their food, and their accommodations, seem generally to have been sometimes excellent, sometimes indifferent, and occasionally abominable. Aaron

Denio, a Canadian, who kept a tavern in Greenfield, Massachu- setts, was described by a town historian as being

of a testy, impatient humor . . . or at any rate sometimes inclined to that mood. On one occasion, when he could not get a satisfactory reply from his wife after he had repeatedly asked her what they were serving for dinner, he seized the pot hanging over the fire, exclaimed "I *vill* know *what* is in that pot," and hastily made his way to the brow of the steep hill back of the house and furiously threw the offending vessel down the hill, and as it went, rolling and tumbling and tossing horribly, mid the steam of the boiling fluid, out came, mingling in dread confusion, pudding, potatoes, pork, beef, cabbage, beets, and turnips, still on it went and on to the bottom of the hill, to the utter dismay and consternation of all peaceable, well-disposed, and good potluck-dinner loving citizens. . . . He gained his point but lost his dinner. Since the days of Don Quixote was never such an adventure undertaken; the attack upon the windmill is not to be mentioned on the same day.

The keeper of one of the early inns in Duxbury, Massachusetts, was another character of some independence; after losing a court case he ordered a new signboard, on which he depicted the officers of the court in caricature, "then stood before his sign and defended his property against the officers who were sent from Boston to remove it."

The theory behind the licensing of taverns was that their keepers would be superior men, responsible citizens, leaders in the community. Indeed many of them seem to have been just that. Ebenezer Crafts, keeper of the principal tavern in Sturbridge, held several town and military offices before going on to found Leicester Academy and the town of Craftsbury, Vermont. One LeBaron of Sutton, Massachusetts, had a flourishing store and a potash business in addition to his tavern. He was "aristocratic, yet cheerful, jovial, and familiar with his customers. He wore his small clothes *à la* the regulation suit for Queen Victoria's receptions: breeches of fine cloth with silver knee buckles, long stockings, and silver shoe buckles. He also wore a cocked hat. He was a gentleman of wealth and high standing." Eli Langley of Waterford, Maine, built the first store in that town, was its first postmaster, and operated a potash work. He was instrumental in laying out the town common and "spent his means freely in building up Waterford." Timothy Keeler of Ridgefield, Connecticut, was an enterprising businessman. He had several flourishing retail and wholesale stores, purchased part of a sloop for the price of one hundred pounds, and owned part of an iron works.

Timothy Dwight pointed out that the reason tavern keepers were such upright, sterling citizens was that the New England colonies and states considered the taverns as "a place where travelers must trust themselves, their horses, luggage, and money; where women as well as men must at times lodge, might need humane and delicate offices, and might be subjected to disagreeable exposures." Every innkeeper had to be recommended by the selectmen, constables, and grand jurors of the town and licensed at the discretion of the court of common pleas. "In consequence of this system, men of no small personal respectability have ever kept inns in this country. Here the contempt with which Englishmen regard this subject is not experienced and is unknown."

John Adams, on the other hand, observed that the spirit of the law was constantly being broken. Justices often were unable to attend the county courts; selectmen had been discouraged by being often disappointed.

Some houses to my knowledge have been licensed which never had any approbation from any selectman. Other persons have been licensed whom the selectmen have found by experience and certified to be guilty of misrule and therefore unfit. Others have been recognized for seven years together without any approbation from the selectmen through that whole time. . . . Those houses have been so shamefully multiplied in the country . . . that decent entertainment for a traveler is nowhere to be had.

Henry Wansey found Mr. Hitchcock of the Brookfield Inn "an intelligent, civil, and cautious man, very inquisitive to know what he could about the passengers, as almost all the landlords are in this country."

The Duc de la Rochefoucault-Liancourt praised the inn kept by a Quaker in Brunswick, Maine.

The guests who frequent his house are not promiscuously mixed together; each different company has its separate sitting, eating, and sleeping rooms; everything bears the appearance of the utmost cleanliness, care, and attention; servants are numerous, and are employed both upon the extensive farm and the business of the inn; the landlord and his wife are persons of good sense, and very obliging in their manner; in short, this inn was a kind of phenomenon of which I never yet saw the counterpart.

When Elias Boudinot stopped at a tavern on the outskirts of New Haven he found that the landlord and his wife had agreed not to take in ladies from the south. "The reason she assigned was the extreme hauteur and uncivil behavior of some ladies from New York." Dr. Mason Cogswell also commented on the difference in manners at Milford in 1826: "A number of very genteel but not refined passengers entered and they seemed as if they were independent. We guessed they must be from the South . . ."

Frances Wright, an English traveler, was surprised at the freedom and independence of New England tavern keepers.

On arriving at a tavern in this country, you excite no kind of *sensation*, come how you will. The master of the house bids you good-day, and you walk in. Breakfast, dinner, and supper are prepared at stated times, to which you must generally contrive to accommodate. There are seldom more hands than enough to dispatch the necessary work. You are not therefore beset by half-a-dozen menials, imagining your wants before you know them yourself; make them known, however, and, if they be rational, they are generally answered with tolerable readiness, and I have invariably found with perfect civility. One thing I must notice, that you are never anywhere charged for attendance. The servant is not yours but the innkeeper's, no demands are made upon you except by the latter. . . . But this arrangement originates in another cause—the republican habits and feelings of the community. I honor the pride which makes a man unwilling to sell his personal service to a fellow creature; to come and go at the beck of another—is it not natural that there should be some unwillingness to do this?

Zadoc Long, a New Englander himself, complained bitterly of a landlord in Weymouth, Massachusetts:

The outward appearance is fair, but within, though the Landlord wear a fashionable coat & hat, & his wife is a handsome, clever thing enough, fit for some place, no doubt, judging from their accommodations they are no better qualified for the business of a publick house than a monkey for a lady's waiter. Stiffened in a certain position within the bar, where he seems inclined to take his ease & where he might be mistaken for a poor painting, the Landlord finds nothing to do for us till it is time to foot the bill, when he takes his pay with as much saucy indifference as if we were still greatly indebted for his services. The lady matches him well.

Timothy Dwight had observed that as a result of the system of licensing in New England "men of no small personal respectability have ever kept inns in this country." But only two decades later Ralph Waldo Emerson was to remark, "In a town everybody puts on airs except the landlord: he is the poor devil, and the commonest sot of a teamster thinks he has the advantage of him."

Besides the ordinary travelers on the road, taverns also catered to special parties, much as inns do today. Sleighing and dancing parties, outings, ordination balls, Fourth of July dinners, sales or vendues, political or judicial meetings, court week if the tavern happened to be in a shire town, and sometimes even funerals were occasions when the tavern was in demand. A historian of Norwich, Connecticut, tells of sleighing parties that ended at the taverns for dinner or other refreshment. The House of Color in Magnolia, Massachusetts, also entertained such parties. Ruth Henshaw, the well-known profilist, in 1796 went on a sleighing party with thirty-five other couples from Leicester to Brookfield. Hezekiah Prince of Camden, Maine, attended just such a party with twelve couples one January afternoon in 1823. Christopher Columbus Baldwin was a member of many such parties in the 1830's. The young ladies of Miss Pierce's seminary in Litchfield also went on evening sleigh rides to country suppers in Goshen, Harwinton, or other nearby villages. At the tavern there they would "order our turkey and oysters, served up with pickles and cake, and then set Black Caesar to play jigs on a cracked fiddle. But the grand occasions were something beyond this, when we got sleighs with five horses, and buffalo-robes and foot-stoves and invited the belles of Litchfield, who never hesitated to go, and set off to the distant village to have a supper and dance."

The teamsters, who made up the largest part of the customers at many taverns, were especially mobile in winter, using sleighs to transport their heavy cargoes of goods. In Keene, New Hampshire, on a single day in January 1844, between sixty and seventy sleighs "loaded with beef, pork, venison, and other country products" passed through on their way to Boston.

Dancing was often performed at the tavern. Indeed by 1800 many if not most of the country inns of New England had ballrooms, although many clergymen still frowned on dancing in their parishes. Jeremy Belknap wrote of New Hampshire in 1812 that at "military musters, at judicial courts, at the raising of houses, at the launching of ships, and at the ordination of

ministers, the young people amused themselves with dancing."
In many communities dancing ended at the curfew hour of
nine, but in others it could go on until midnight or later. Tavern
refreshments for dances often consisted of "fruits, nuts, cake,
and wine or cider." Christopher Columbus Baldwin visited
Hopkinton Springs, Massachusetts, in 1832 with a group of
friends. "We started at eight in the morning and reached Brigham's, in Westboro, about ten, where we had strawberries and
cream, with ice and soda. We arrived at the Springs about
twelve and spent the whole day in rolling ninepins, swinging,
waltzing, playing bagatelle, bathing, and the like. The ladies
mingled in all our sports."

At the House of Color dancing parties arrived by sleigh in
winter and by hayrack in summer. "There were minuets,
stately country dances, and games such as blind man's buff and
spin the cover. . . . Square dances, including quadrilles, contra
dances, money musk and Virginia reels were most fashionable.
It is told of one of the old Puritans that so dexterous was he on
his feet that he held aloft a cup of tea and saucer as he whirled
about without spilling a drop."

Always at Thanksgiving time there were turkey shoots at
the taverns. Ruth Henshaw's brother William attended one in
1805 and brought home the family's Thanksgiving bird. There
were also animal exhibitions and contests of various kinds:
one Mr. Hooker of Farmington, Connecticut, in 1820 took his
two small children to Phelps Inn to see "a large tawny lion,
a tall and beautiful Persian llama, an ostrich, and two or three
monkeys . . . John rode the llama around the barn, while the
keeper led the animal and I steadied the rider." Hezekiah Prince
of Camden attended several such exhibitions, "a caravan of
wild animals . . . an elephant, a lion, tiger, camel, leopard, bear,
wolf, and a number of monkeys and other animals." Sweetser's
Tavern in Chester, New Hampshire, exhibited the first elephant
in that town in 1816; Warner's first was at Daniel George's in
1829. Occasionally there would be a bear, dog, or cock fight, or,
as in Hartford at the Eagle Hotel in 1819, a fight "between
the buffaloe and eight or ten of the best dogs that can be procured in this city." Sometimes, as at the celebration of the beheading of Louis XVI in 1793 or the signing of the peace
treaty in 1815, an ox would be roasted for the people's de-

light. Fourth of July dinners were also commonly held at taverns.

Many taverns had bowling alleys, as did the inn at Hopkinton Springs. Christopher Columbus Baldwin spent many happy afternoons there playing ninepins. Hezekiah Prince rolled ninepins at an inn in Thomaston, Maine. Occasionally hunting parties stopped at taverns for refreshment and amusement. The taverns were taxed to capacity on muster day, when, not content with the liquors sold on the field, both officers and men retired to the taverns, often not leaving them until early morning.

When courts were held in any town, the inns served not only as hotels for the members of the bench and bar but also as convivial gathering places in the evening. Many bills for court expenses, including food, drink, and stabling and feed for horses, still survive. Sometimes prisoners were locked in chambers in the tavern while their presence was not required in court for the moment. Court week was a busy time for the landlord, who must staff and stock the bar, have all his rooms ready, and prepare meals for many extra people. In the early days before towns erected courthouses, a tavern room would often serve as courtroom.

Newspaper advertisements give us some clue to the service provided by taverns. A New London, Connecticut, inn of 1770 provided "good attendance with plain diet," at five pounds per week. Isaac Marsh's Coachman and Farmer's Tavern in Dunstable, New Hampshire, in 1805 could accommodate twenty ladies and gentlemen, sixty horses and oxen, and "can house fifteen carriages and loaded wagons where they will be dry and secure." The Steam-Boat Hotel in New Haven, not infrequently the scene of yellow fever epidemics, boasted: "Gentlemen and ladies who may visit the seashore for their health can be accommodated in no better situation . . . as it directly fronts the Sound, in full view of all vessels passing and repassing, and during the summer season is delightfully situated to receive refreshing breezes from the sea." The City Hotel, Hartford, in 1819 served "the best vitals and liquors which the market affords, at moderate prices. Travelers will find a quiet house, good rooms, clean and comfortable beds, and attention to their commands."

Jacob Coffin's Inn in Londonderry, New Hampshire, in 1806 advertised a stable

open to receive carriages which may pass through without unharnessing, and affords the best of hay and provender; twenty sleighs can be accommodated in case of a storm. His house will give the traveler a good fire in winter, and clean rooms and beds both summer and winter; his larder will be supplied with the best of provisions the country affords; here the weary traveler may rest on a bed of down, or does he want a glass of wine or spirit of almost any kind for his stomach sake, it is here at hand.

Samuel Nott of Amherst, New Hampshire, was prepared "to board at court and other times, to entertain dancing and other parties, having an excellent hall, to provide public entertainment, and to accommodate travelers to their satisfaction." A fellow landlord in the same town had stables "new made very convenient both for the accommodation of horses and ox-teams . . . good hay, agreeable vitals and drink, comfortable fires, clean beds, ready attendance, and reasonable charges." Apollos Hitchcock in Hartford offered "the choicest liquors of every kind usual in the best houses—meats, vegetables, and fruits, the best the market affords, clean beds, civil treatment, and an orderly house."

The earliest colonial legislation required taverns to hang out signs, and this practice continued well into the nineteenth century. Many of the old signs are well known, such as Boston's "Bunch of Grapes," "Bell in Hand," "Lamb," "King's Head," and "Green Dragon"; Salem's "Bell"; Newburyport's "Blue Anchor" and "[General] Wolfe." Edward Everett Hale recalled many of the signs of his youth:

These country taverns always had signs, generally swinging from a post with a cross-bar in front of the house. The sign might be merely the name of the keeper . . . more probably it was the picture of the American eagle or of a rising sun. Neptune rising from the sea was a favorite device. I remember at Worcester the elephant. . . . there remain some General Washingtons. After I was a man I had occasion to travel a good deal one summer in Northern Vermont, where the tavern signs still existed. Almost without exception their devices were of the American eagle with his wings spread, or of the American eagle holding the English lion in chains, or of the lion chained without any American eagle. These were held in memory of Macomb's and McDonough's victories at Plattsburg and on the lake. They also, perhaps, referred to the fact that most of these taverns were supported by the wagons of smugglers, who in their good, large peddlers' carts, provided themselves with English goods in Canada, which they sold on our side of the line. In our generation one is more apt to see a tavern sign in a museum than hanging on a gallows-tree.

What of the drinking that went on in the taverns? Historians, travelers, diarists and journalists, clergymen, observers of the social scene all tell us that it was heavy from the beginning and continued heavy until the temperance movement put an end to it in the mid-nineteenth century. Magistrates and ministers in the seventeenth century complained that contrary to the intent of the law townspeople were congregating in the taverns in the evening and even on the Sabbath and lecture day. They tried to put teeth into legislation by requiring landlords to allow a man to drink only half an hour at a time, not to serve him when he was drunk, not to serve Indians at all, and to close during the hours of church service as well as promptly every evening. Nothing had any effect, not even strict observance of the law by conscientious landlords. Whether it was the custom of the day, the tedium of their daily lives, the extremes of the New England climate, or whatever, all men drank, many of them heavily.

There were several drinks that were favorites at the taverns in addition to the ever-present rum, brandy, and cider. Flip was made usually of beer, rum, sugar or other sweetening, and water. A red-hot toddy iron would be plunged into the beer, then the rum, sugar, and water added. Occasionally eggs were part of the flip recipe. Most taverns kept the iron constantly in the fire. "Half a pint of beer to a quart of rum was considered to be the right proportions." Punch, made of rum, sugar, water, and lemon or lime juice, was a great favorite, and many were the bowls of punch consumed at an evening gathering. Grog was rum, infrequently gin, mixed with water. Toddy was a milk mixture. Cider and cider brandy were most popular with country people. Wines, chiefly port and Madeira, were served as dinner drinks.

John Quincy Adams, when a law student at Newburyport, visited a tavern with a friend one evening in 1787. The two young men were tired after a long day of reading Blackstone and copying legal forms, and they supped at the tavern on "birds." Three acquaintances joined them. "We got to singing

after supper, and the bottle went around with an unusual rapid-
ity, until a round dozen had disappeared. I then thought it was
high time to retreat, and with some difficulty slipped away from
those of the company who appeared to be the most inspired."

The Duc de la Rochefaucault-Liancourt observed that in
Maine the commonest tavern drink was grog, whereas forty
years earlier James Birket found that in Portsmouth, New
Hampshire, it was cider and rum. To the historian of Weare,
New Hampshire, William Little, it was straight rum.

No man could run a grocery store without keeping a barrel on tap in the back
room, where all customers could help themselves. At all trainings and musters,
bridge raisings and the like, the town furnished the rum. At all ordinations,
installations, councils and other great religious meetings, the church provided it.
Ministers treated all who called upon them, and apologized for not having more
and better stimulants. Church members and all others treated the minister when
he called, and he often went home at night very boozy. The odor of rum was
sure to be present at all town meetings, raisings, sheep washings and shearings,
huskings, and log-rollings. It was common at funerals, and the decanter and
glasses were often placed on the head of the coffin as a token of the liberality
of the mourners.

The citizens of Harvard, Massachusetts, came daily to the
town's two taverns, according to a local history,

from all the districts of the town, on foot, a-horseback, in every variety of
vehicle—some bringing butter and eggs or other domestic produce to exchange
for a few groceries and a jug of New England rum; some coming empty handed
to kill time and soak themselves with toddy and flip. Especially in the long
autumn and winter evenings would the sanded floors of the barrooms become
the arena where a concourse of boon companions, in an atmosphere blue with
tobacco smoke and profanity, wrangled about political questions, played practical jokes upon each other, told ribald stories, sang ribald songs, and guzzled
until stupid or half crazed. About midnight, locked out by the landlord, these
free American citizens would reel to their half-starved, shivering steeds tied
nearby, and drive howling home to add to the discomfort and misery there.

In Simsbury, Connecticut, weddings, social calls, and militia
training days were additional occasions for heavy imbibing.
"At eleven o'clock a.m. and at four o'clock p.m. mechanics
regularly took their grog. No farmer could reap his harvest or
finish his haying without a keg of rum. In winter it was warming and in summer it was cooling." Samuel Griswold Good-

rich, the noted writer, called the practice of drinking at the taverns "tavern haunting." Fisher Ames, that somewhat jaundiced Federalist, was irked at seeing "a Dedham tavern made the scene of frolic and flip on so many occasions. A gingerbeer lottery, a vendue, a dance, a singing meeting, a sleigh ride, everything filled with young fellows, and our apprentice boys already claimed the rights of men against their masters."

Christopher Columbus Baldwin and a friend took two young ladies on an afternoon jaunt one fine day in 1833. "We stayed at Whitcomb's Tavern about an hour and drank mulled wine, a kind of stupefying beverage made of eggs, sugar, and hot wine." On another occasion, when his sleighing party stopped at a tavern "mulled wine was prepared for the ladies and flip for the gentlemen, but by mistake the flip was carried to the ladies, and they do not find their error until our flip is nearly gone, when they pronounced it very unpleasant stuff!!"

This picture began to change after 1825, when first the clergy, then wiser heads among the citizenry began to see that a bad practise was growing worse and that New England was becoming a region of drunkards. What began as a movement toward temperance after 1840 became one for total abstinence. At first towns began to curtail the liquor sold by the drink in stores and grog shops. They then turned their criticism if not their bylaws against the taverns. Voluntary temperance became the fashion. Farmers began chopping down their apple orchards. Cider began disappearing from the dinner table, and it began to be somewhat of a social error for one to visit the tavern too frequently. By 1840 Emerson could record in his journal, after a walk to Stowe with Nathaniel Hawthorne, "The temperance society emptied the barroom. It is a cold place."

Taverns continued, however, if not as sources of excessive conviviality, as houses catering to strangers and travelers. Stages still stopped, even though railroad hotels were beginning to appear on the scene. "In front of the tavern [according to one traveler] stood great carts filled with spinning wheels for country trade, wagons filled with common household furniture and all things necessary for a new settlement, peddlars' carts of every description, and stock drovers." But now travelers could complain of things other than bad food, uncomfort-

able beds, poor lodging, and much drinking. By 1835 Harriet
Martineau was noting disapprovingly that

in these small inns the disagreeable practice of rocking in the chair is seen in its
excess. In the inn parlor are three or four rocking chairs, in which sit ladies who
are vibrating in different directions, and at various velocities, as to try the head
of a stranger almost as severely as the tobacco-chewer his stomach. How this
lazy and ungraceful indulgence ever became general, I cannot imagine; but the
nation seems so wedded to it, that I see little chance of its being forsaken.

But the simpler pleasures remained. One could, like Ruth
Henshaw, pass a pleasant evening with friends in a tavern
parlor with the simple entertainment of "wine, apples, pears,
cracked nuts, raisins, and, at ten, preserved quinces and cream
—cards, checkers, backgammon." One could stop for an afternoon bite, as did Sarah Connell Ayer, a Maine housewife, and
be served "apple pie and cheese," or find, after a tedious day-
long journey extending into late evening, "milk punch and
crackers and a good fire." One could occasionally dine sumptu-
ously on "roast goose, roast pea-hen, baked stuffed venison,
beef, and pork." One could, after a long visit in Virginia, find
at a tavern just over the threshold of New England, "brown
bread & cyder, . . . not seen for seven months." If one were dis-
trustful by nature, as was Justice Oliver Wendell, and "revolted
at the barbarism of country taverns, one could carry one's
own freshly killed chicken under the seat of the carriage," de-
liver it "to the cook of the Wayside Inn" at the end of twenty-
four hours and have another put in its place "to undergo a like
seasoning."

The Village Tavern

The Village Tavern was erected in 1946–47, as soon after
World War II as construction materials could be allocated
and workers secured. It was badly needed both as a service
building to provide food and rest to visitors and as an exhibition
area for collections that could not be housed elsewhere. Because a large structure was needed and the cost of locating,
moving, and re-erecting such a building was prohibitive for the
Village budget at that time, it was decided to put up a modern

structure, in keeping with the architecture of the Village as a whole but containing modern kitchens, dining facilities, rest rooms, and exhibit areas. Since then the Village staff has thought wistfully of an authentic tavern of the past, the one structure that would complete the Green, and no doubt some-day the Green will be graced by a fine old tavern of the early nineteenth century. The present one will remain to fulfill the purpose for which it was set up.

The plan developed by architect John Radford Abbott is an adaptation of that of several old inns. The ell, including the Great Room, had been part of Albert B. Wells' summer home at Mashapaug, Connecticut. The basement dining room was installed in 1950; the rear dining areas on the first floor were set up in 1964 and those on the second floor in 1968. The arched ceiling beams of the Great Room come from a covered bridge over the Sacandaga River, Fish House, New York.

To the right of the front door is the tavern office. Here is the innkeeper's bar, his key and letter racks, his shelves filled with candlesticks for travelers to carry on their way to bed. In one corner is a cupboard filled with English and Dutch delft-ware, an appealing tin-enamel glazed earthenware of the seven-teenth and eighteenth centuries. In the cupboard is a finely cut basket made probably in Dublin, a wonderful posset pot dating perhaps from the 1690's, a heavy dish with the portrait of a sad-faced, rather toothachy monarch on it, bottles, bowls, plates, vases, and candlesticks. The shelves on one side of the fireplace display some of the historical blue Staffordshire so popular in the early nineteenth century. A sugar bowl decorated with a cottage scene sits side by side with a view of the Boston Statehouse, and Mount Vernon vies for attention with Wash-ington on horseback. Maps of Massachusetts and of the king's dominions in North America and a print of the "Venetian Lady at Masquerade" hang on the walls. The drover's bed, a long, hard bench with chest below, sits against the back wall. It was on beds such as these, right in the barroom, that the men who drove their cattle to market slept when they stopped overnight at a wayside tavern.

The lounge beyond is furnished with sofas and chairs so that visitors may stop for a few minutes' rest. Country wing chairs, Empire sofas, a piano made by John Osborne of Boston, and a curly-maple highboy make up the balance of its furnishings, while the walls are lined with country portraits, among them that of Stephen Fitch of Norwalk, Connecticut, undoubtedly a distant relative of Stephen Fitch of Windham, whose house now stands in Old Sturbridge Village.

Opposite the office is the Schaefer Bar, gift of the R. J. Schaefer Foundation. The small tables, Windsor, slat, and spindle-back chairs, and settle are the appurtenances of a bar that in its day would have been devoted solely to the refreshment of the male, travelers and townsmen alike. The prints on the wall are those typical of barrooms of the early nineteenth century: the Battle of Lexington, George Washington, a map of Massachusetts, and "The Life and Age of Man." The walls have stenciled borders, the fireplace is usually lighted in cool weather, and the room radiates good cheer. Here the visitor may order a rum shrub, a toddy, or a glass of ale.

Beyond the bar, in the Great Room, are two massive fireplaces, one by a window, an unusual feature. The walls are decorated with carved and painted eagles. One dining parlor behind has the sign of Moses Smith, innkeeper, over its fireplace. The corner cupboard in the other contains Staffordshire pieces commemorating the memory of Lafayette—the landing scene and one depicting him mourning at Franklin's tomb. (Lafayette enshrined himself in the hearts of New Englanders when as an old man and accompanied by his son he made a tour of that region as part of a visit to this nation in 1824–25.)

On the second floor is the body of the Village art collection, which for the most part consists of country art, that of the little-trained or self-trained artist, the itinerant, the artisan or tradesman-cum-painter, the schoolgirl artist, the housewife who painted in her spare time. In this collection one may see pastel portraits by Ruth Henshaw Bascom, a minister's wife who painted largely to oblige her friends and neighbors; the work of William Matthew Prior, who attained a certain fame and opened a studio in Boston; portraits by Benjamin Greenleaf, Gerrit Schipper, Erastus Salisbury Field, S. A. and R. W. Shute, Joseph H. Davis, and William F. Ainsworth. Here also are fine watercolors by Richard Brunton and John Coles. The painting and stenciling of coach painters and other artisans are shown in the painted window shades, bed, bench, bellows, table, boxes, and looking glass at the end of the hall. Schoolgirls—and a few boys—and young lady artists are represented by paintings on velvet, needlework and watercolor paintings, watercolor mourning pictures and family records, a few chalk and charcoal scenes. One may also see some of the equipment of these students and parlor artists—boxes of watercolors, sets of drawing and sketching tools, sketch books, instruction books, and stencil patterns. Painted fireboards and panels, genre paintings, and a few pieces of sculpture—among them a statue of Ceres attributed to Simeon Skillin, Jr., and a bust of Washington attributed to Samuel McIntire—complete the exhibition.

The basement is at present a dining room and cafeteria. It too contains special exhibitions: a fine collection of woodenware ranging from butter prints and molds to tankards, mortars and pestles, and huge burl bowls; a cupboard full of English creamware including mugs and pitchers with the Farmer's Arms decoration, a jug commemorating the fine art of drinking, and a decorated mug dated 1776; and several shelves of lusterware and children's mugs.

Painted chests and wallboards.

The Village Center 7

Miner Grant's General Store

The general store was the unit of commodity exchange in most rural New England communities. Many towns had two, three, four or more of these establishments, and occasionally a West India goods store, a hardware store, a dry goods store, or a milliner's as well. Tolland, Connecticut, which in 1804 had a population of about 1,600, had "one apothecary's shop & 3 or 4 stores of goods."

In the early nineteenth century many New England farmers still subsisted in part at least on a barter economy. The surplus products of their farms—their cheeses, butter, grain, hides, tallow, pork, beef, wood ashes, and the products of the women's hands, their knitted stockings, caps, and mittens, their woven ticking, linens, and towels, and their candles—could all be sold at the local store or taken by wagon or sleigh to Boston, Portsmouth, New Haven, or other market towns. David Boardman of New Milford, Connecticut, advertised that he purchased for cash or barter "pot-ash, pork, beef, butter, wheat, rye, corn, oats, flax-seed, bees-wax, bar-iron, nail-rods, geese-feathers, hog's lard, tallow, and furrs of all kinds."

When they took their produce to market, farmers were gen-

Miner Grant's General Store.

erally paid in cash, but at the general store in their own village they usually bartered—so much cheese, so many hides, or so many pounds of pork for sugar, salt, coffee, tea, spices, dry goods, or whatever. Thus the storekeeper's account book would have both a debit and a credit side, and only once a year or so would he add up his accounts and see where he stood in relation to each customer. Delinquents would then be urged to pay up, while others might find they had enough credit to indulge in the purchase of a bit of finery, a longed-for tea set, or a clock complete with patent works.

The store might be a room in the merchant's house, an ell or section added to his house, a room in a building along the main street, or a separate building in its own right. Country stores varied in size from tiny to fairly substantial, from a room to a whole building. The one thing they had in common was the universality of their stock. They sold literally everything that could be sold—and then some.

Lucius Loring, who kept a store in Brookfield, Maine, about the year 1820, took [in] little or no money. We took oats, beans, peas, butter, two cloth, flannel cloth, flannel cloth, &. Why I have taken [sic] three and a half tons of butter in a single summer and autumn at ten cents a pound. It was hard getting anything out of it at that price. We used to get a big profit on our goods and that helped out. For two or three years after Ralph Jewett and I went into trade together, we sold $20,000 a year of dry goods. We had customers from up as far as Jay and from over to Paris Cape. We built what is called the Loring Store the year that the railroad was built, and it cost us $1600. The first year we paid for the store, supported two families, and in addition to this a net profit of $2600. That is the best business I ever did in a single year. We bought prints in Boston at ten cents a yard and sold for a shilling. . . . the people then had no expensive habits. They didn't go into luxuries, and were frugal and saving. Their dress and living was plain.

The extent of general-store merchandise may be gleaned from the newspaper advertisements of the day. They carried groceries, wines, and liquors; dry goods; hardware, tools, and cutlery; earthenware and crockery; glassware, tinware, and ironware; apothecary herbs, drugs, and patent medicines of all kinds. "Lay out a dollar when you come, and you shall have a glass of Rum," but "Since man to man is so unjust, 'Tis hard to say whom I can trust; I've trusted many to my sorrow; pay me today, I'll trust tomorrow."

Many storekeepers had a side business selling potash. They took in the farmers' ashes for cash or credit, converted them to potash, and sold it in the market town. Stores-cum-potash works were legion throughout New England.

In the collections at Old Sturbridge Village is the 1791 store inventory of Josiah Fairbank of Sterling, Massachusetts. He stocked buckles of pewter, brass, silver, and silver plate for both kneebreeches and shoes of every material, slates and pencils, hats, soap, ink, books (the Bible, Watt's Psalms, school texts, sermons, pamphlets, *New Cruso* [*Robinson Crusoe*]), paper, combs, hardware, snuffers and candlesticks, tinware and china- ware, cards for carding wool, sheep and calf skins, flowers and plumes for hats, foot and hand spinning wheels, sieves, bed cords, rum, brandy, gin, and wine, groceries, tallow, loaf and pigtail tobacco, snuff, copper, glass, spices, canes, whips, toast- ers, glassware, pewter vessels, dry goods, yarn and tow stock- ings, men's and ladies' gloves, shawls, handkerchiefs, threads, spectacles, pins, fiddle strings, snuff and tobacco boxes, powder flasks, basket bottoms, buttons, casks and kegs, scales, weights,

Interior of the store.

wooden and tin measures, desks, chests, boxes, cannisters, chairs, and some farm-produced items—butter, cheese, corn, wheat, and potash.

Storekeepers occasionally traded at a distance and also did some wholesale business. Sometimes the storekeeper specialized in hardware, dry goods, tools, or drugs.

The doors, shutters, and clapboards of the store were often plastered with notices of various kinds: vendues, auctions, forced sales, creditors' and debtors' notices, reports of runaway apprentices, stray cattle, horses, and sheep, lotteries, town

A corner of the store.

meetings, courts, elections, town bylaws, and state laws. The
front of the store usually carried all nonliquid merchandise.
At the rear men could buy liquor by the gallon, quart, pint,
or single drink. When they could purchase by the drink, the
store qualified also as a grog shop. Here were barrels, bottles,
wine pipes, and hogsheads. The counter might have a few
tumblers, bottles, and a toddy stick. Sometimes there were
chairs and a fireplace here, at which one could sit warming his
exterior while his drink warmed his interior. One historian recalled:

A New England grocery store that did not have a hogshead of West India rum on tap, beside the hogshead of Porto Rica molasses, was most unusual and unpopular. My grandfather's store was no exception to the general rule, and the hogshead of rum was there on tap, with a gill dipper hanging on a nail driven in the head of the hogshead. A customer would frequently take down the gill dipper, fill it with rum, and after drinking it would pass the clerk a penny, which he considered ample pay for the same.

At a Jaffrey, New Hampshire, store there was a board nailed to a post on which each man put down his own account and paid when he could.

Storekeepers occasionally were town postmasters as well. They were usually enterprising individuals, trading in land, lumber, and furs as well as their store stock. Not infrequently they owned and operated farms. They took their turn at serving in the hierarchy of town offices and were most often valued citizens. Some idea of their quality, as well as the qualities they sought in others, can be seen from an advertisement for a store apprentice that appeared in the *Connecticut Courant* in 1793: "A lad . . . honest, healthy, active, obliging, and naturally diligent; who can write and cypher, and is full willing not to assume the Buck or Man of Pleasure till he is out of his apprenticeship, as the person that wants him expects he will attend to business."

The Duc de la Rochefaucault-Liancourt commented that New England stores "in places thinly inhabited" were shops "where all kinds of commodities intended for consumption are to be found, and sold by retail; nothing is excluded from [them]; here are candles and matches, as well as stuff and tape." The duke was accustomed to the more specialized shops and boutiques of his native land.

Miner Grant's store was purchased and re-erected at Old Sturbridge Village in 1939. Its early history is obscure, but it appears to have been built in Stafford, Connecticut, about 1790. Miner Grant sold his store in nearby Willington in 1802 and purchased this structure from Dr. Samuel Willard, a leading physician of Stafford who was associated with the spa at Stafford Springs, where John Adams was an occasional visitor. Grant operated the store with his son, Miner Grant, Jr., for a few years; then it was operated by Miner, Jr., and his brother Billings. Like all country storekeepers, Miner Grant and his

sons accepted payments in kind, "any kind of produce . . . also
clover seed, beef, pork, flannel, and tow cloth . . . butter, cheese,
mittens and stockings." They seem to have specialized in dyes,
paints, and drugs and medicines, and they advertised their
wares as far away as Hartford. They patronized local industry
as well, carrying Stafford hollowware (iron). Their wines were
perhaps a little more expensive than those of most country
dealers, including Madeira, port, sherry, Lisbon, "London Par-
ticulars," tenerife, and Malaga. Their dry goods were perhaps
run-of-the-mill, but their drugs included "Wheaton's, Rawson's
and Wood's Bitters, Anderson's and Lockyer's Pills, Hooper's
Female Pills, Lee's, Rawson's and Sutton's Female Pills, Balsam Life Steer's Opodeldoc, Bateman's Drops, Godfrey's Cor-
dial, Balsam, Honey, Dalby's Carminative, British Orals, Ce-
phalic Snuff, Fraunce's Elixir, Essence of Peppermint, and
Worm Powder."

Miner Grant was born in 1756 in Stonington, Connecticut,
not far from New London. He lived in Mansfield, Willington,
Stafford, and Ashford before migrating west to New York
State, where he died in 1828. One story has it that he was a
physician, and he may indeed have had the title of "Doctor."
His possible interest in medicine would account for his extensive stock of drugs, said to have been the best on the turnpike
between New York and Boston. Miner Grant, Jr., maintained
the store until his death in 1850, and the firm remained in the
Grant family until 1892. Miner Grant, Jr., also operated an
iron foundry with his brother, two members of a family named
Hyde, and Ezra White.

The front room of the store today looks as it might have in
the early nineteenth century. Shelves are crowded with merchandise—dry goods, crockery, pewter, tin, ironware, brass,
drugs and patent medicines, ink bottles and inkwells, books,
stationery, mittens and stockings, tea and coffee, and scores of
other items. Barrels, kegs, bins, and boxes stand on the floor,
while hanging on walls and from overhead hooks and on
shelves near the ceiling are trunks, bandboxes, skates and snowshoes, tea boxes, cages, traps, warming pans, baskets, and
many other stock items. On the counter are eggs in tin baskets
as though just brought in for sale, cheese, butter, dyestuffs,
and those articles that moved most quickly or were perishable.

In the room at the rear are a few reproductions and present-day articles on sale to visitors—the ubiquitous postcards and film, a few Village publications, flour from the Gristmill, cans of New England baked beans, corn chowder, and Indian pudding, baskets, wooden bowls, mortars and pestles, crockery, and penny candy. Dearest of all to the hearts of child visitors is the candy: old-fashioned lemon, lime, and horehound drops, rock candy, peppermint and cinnamon sticks, lozenges, comfits. Here are a few of the smells that once made up the atmosphere of a country store—smells of spices, liquors, coffee beans, mint, and occasionally the all-pervading odor of new-smoked cod.

The assault on today's civilization is largely on our ears and our eyes—the roar of traffic and machinery, the ugliness of billboards and car graveyards, and the squalor of our streets. That of early America was chiefly on the sense of smell— decaying garbage and sewage in streets, manure in barnyards and roads, pungent dyestuffs, the acrid odors of the tanneries and fisheries, and the combination of smells from unsealed vessels in the general store. Not all were unpleasant but most were strong, and their memory lingers into the present.

The Bank

During the colonial period there were no banks as such in this country. Many of the provinces coined money, most speculated in land, but the standard to which they were held to account in payment of debt was the British pound sterling, of which they saw very little. In the course of the conflict with Britain, the Continental Congress realized the need for a stable banking operation and in 1781 established the Bank of North America in Philadelphia. After the adoption of the Federal Constitution in 1789 and establishment of the Bank of the United States, banks began springing up all over New England. According to the census of 1800 there were then seventeen in the region, one in every town with a population of more than 5,000. By 1826 Connecticut alone had thirteen banks, and there were 157 in all New England.

The Thompson Bank was built in Thompson, Connecticut, a small community in Windham County that had separated from the town of Killingly in 1785. Thompson was a small but thriving industrial and commercial community when several of its most prominent citizens applied for a bank charter in 1833. Its population was about 3,000. It had two good rivers, the French and the Quinebaug, which made possible an early development of cotton and wool spinning and weaving mills and a hat manufactory. There were also shoemaking shops, tailoring shops, a milliner's shop, a jeweler's shop, a retail arcade, and a temperance general store. At frequent intervals, though never for long, the town had its own newspaper, as well as taverns, stables, law offices, and many other establishments. Turnpikes from Hartford to the Rhode Island line and from Rhode Island to Dudley and on to Boston and Springfield ran through the town.

The Thompson Bank.

The bank president's office.

Among the men who secured a bank charter from the State of Connecticut were Harvey Blashfield, who had an interest in the Stone Chapel textile factory; Robert Grosvenor, physician and part owner of the Killingly Manufacturing Company; William H. Mason, part owner of the Thompson Manufacturing Company, a cotton mill known irreverently as the Swamp Factory; John Nichols, part owner of the Connecticut Manufacturing Company (a cotton-spinning factory) and one-time postmaster; Talcott Crosby, who operated a general store and was a probate judge; Jonathan Nichols, county surveyor and probate judge; William Fisher, who owned a cotton-spinning factory and would hire only temperance workers; William Reed, owner of the Brick Factory for cotton spinning; and Simon Davis, lawyer and postmaster.

The Thompson Bank was duly incorporated with a capital stock of $80,000. Harvey Blashfield was elected its first president and Joseph D. Gay cashier. The directors erected the building, probably in 1835, at a cost of somewhat under $2,000. Bank notes were printed, two of which are now in the Village collections. The bank struggled along for a couple of years, barely survived the Panic of 1837, and then, at first falteringly, forged ahead to become a thriving institution.

Connecticut banks had the unenviable reputation of lending disproportionately large sums of money to their own directors, thus operating as a kind of closed corporation. The Thompson Bank was probably no exception in this statewide custom; certainly it played an important part in the industrial expansion of the town. In 1865, following the financial upheaval of the Civil War, it became a national bank. Thompson suffered after this date, however. The Norwich and Worcester Railroad had bypassed it; its turnpikes were no longer heavily traveled; and stagecoach lines were discontinued. The small mills closed, one by one. Nearby Putnam organized a bank of its own. In 1893, in an effort to save it, the directors moved the Thompson Bank to Putnam, but six years later they had to close its doors. The bank building was sold to the town of Thompson, which used it as a depository for town records and as a courtroom for the trial of minor cases. In the 1940's, having outlived its public usefulness, it was turned over to the Eastern Connecticut Council, Boy Scouts of America, who eventually gave it to Old Sturbridge Village. The Village presented the land on which it stood to the Congregational Church of Thompson, Inc., and erected a new building for the Boy Scouts.

The architectural style of the Thompson Bank is Greek Revival. John Warner Barber sketched the building on the Thompson common soon after its erection and recorded for posterity the parapet that was severely damaged in the hurricane of 1938 and later removed. The building is of brick con-

struction, but its front is stucco scribed to look like ashlar cement and painted to look like Connecticut sandstone. The portico, columns, and parapet give it the appearance of a small and modest Greek temple set down in the New England countryside. Windows and doors have heavy iron shutters, doubtless for reasons of security; tradition has it that a robbery of this bank was once attempted. The tin roof is a replacement.

The Greek-temple illusion is heightened somewhat when one steps inside and sees cornice, frieze, and paint colors, but here it ends. Clearly the single room and alcove were meant for business. The vault, a replacement of the original, is at the right rear and is built of heavy granite blocks. Here were kept deposits and bank notes, mortgages, securities, and all records not currently in use. The vault doors are heavy wrought iron. Beyond the vault, on the side wall, is the teller's counter, which is painted and grained to stimulate rosewood. Here and at the clerk's desk beyond was transacted all the ordinary business of deposit and withdrawal.

The bank client could wait his turn with the teller simply by sitting at ease on the pine settee opposite, and after completing his business he might walk through the archway and past the oak-grained divider that separates the main room from the president's office and settle himself for a confidential chat about the need for railroad business, the precarious financial position of one of the mills, or the desirability of securing a loan to finance the purchase of additional land, a larger building, or newer machinery. This office is comfortably furnished with a mahogany and walnut desk, an Empire bookcase holding ledgers and daybooks, a square Empire table, and armchairs. Here the directors met monthly, here a merchant or manufacturer of some local consequence would be invited to sit while his loan was being negotiated or while he and the president talked about Jackson's insane attitude toward the National Bank, the danger of speculation in the West, or the state of the Nation in general. Here no doubt the Panic of 1837 was anxiously ridden out, and here were signed the documents that made the Thompson Bank a national bank. On the floor is a Scotch ingrain carpet, on the wall a Simon Willard regulator clock, and on the table an astral lamp dating from the 1830's.

The building seems always to have been heated by a wood

stove. The handsome chandelier hanging from the ceiling, brass treated to look like gold, is an Argand type and burns whale oil. It was made by a New York firm. The walls are plastered and painted a light gray, the ceiling white. The cornice is brown accented in gold and the frieze is stenciled gray anthemia on a brown ground.

These two buildings, the General Store and the Bank, represent all that existed of formal commercial activity in rural communities of the early nineteenth century. Although the general stores multiplied and there may have been one or two specialized shops, many small towns managed without a bank. Most farmers probably never entered a bank, for these institutions did not act as savings banks or extend long-term credit loans at low interest. No one was encouraged to deposit and no interest was paid on savings. The chief business of the bank was short-term lending and issuing notes.

For this reason the bank was both a convenience and a necessity to the new industrialists, the small mill and shop owners, and the railroad and turnpike men, but of little use to farmers except for those few who were able to negotiate loans and repay on time. The store, on the other hand, was patronized by all, and the cotton magnate who purchased his groceries and household needs in cash was here no better known than the farmer who paid by barter. Together these institutions paved the way for the larger commercial transactions at banks and the purely cash or credit transactions in stores that were to become common after 1850.

The Printing Office

The Village Printing Office is the little office used by the famed Worcester printer and publisher Isaiah Thomas. Thomas moved to Worcester in the opening days of the Revolution, secretly carrying his press out of British-occupied Boston. There in the last two decades of the eighteenth century he operated one of the most renowned printing establishments of the day.

He built his printing office, complete with presses and banks of type, on Court House Hill in 1782. Two years later he allowed Edward Bangs, a rising young attorney, to erect on the

The Isaiah Thomas Printing Office.

property a small office thirty-one by seventeen feet. In later years Thomas used this small building as a counting room and office and for a while had a bookstore here. A few years after his death in 1831 the property was sold. The little office was moved opposite the Worcester Rural Cemetery, was purchased by the Cemetery Association in 1853, and in the 1860's acquired a mansard roof. It was presented to the Village by the Trustees of the Worcester Rural Cemetery in 1951, moved to Sturbridge, and opened the following year.

Although no printing was ever done in this building during

Thomas' lifetime, it was decided to set it up as a printer's office of the early nineteenth century. In the front room to the left of the entrance is an eighteenth-century wooden press on which Thomas himself may have worked when he was briefly employed by Daniel Fowle in Portsmouth, New Hampshire, in the late 1760's. This press is on permanent loan from the Society for the Preservation of New England Antiquities. It is a screw press, with wooden frame, bed, beam, and platen. It uses sheepskin-covered inking balls and hand type. On just such a press Thomas must have printed the first issues of his newspaper, the *Massachusetts Spy*, in Boston and later in Worcester.

The room opposite has been set up as a bookstore. Thomas was noted for fine printing, and in his bookstore he sold his own publications as well as many others. In the 1780's his stock was so diversified as to include stationery, legal blanks of various kinds, writing paper, ink, inkwells and pots, sealing wax and wafers, slates and slate pencils, pocketbooks, razor straps, and wallpaper. After 1800 he started listing his book inventory, volumes of "history, voyages, travels, geography, philosophy, divinity, law, physic, surgery, anatomy, arts, sciences, husbandry, architecture, mathematics, miscellanies, poetry, novels, antiquities, sacred music, &c." He frequently had on hand 6,000 copies of his "standing Bible," in sheets only, ready for binding. When one glances around the bookstore one can see the same kind of stock he once carried: a few hundred volumes of poetry, literature, history, philosophy, and religion; slates and slate pencils, quills and quill holders and tools for making quills, spectacles, pocketbooks, leather trunks and boxes, scales and weights, paint boxes, globes, jewelry, and reams of paper. On the walls are copperplate engravings for sale: a portrait of Washington, Napoleon on his steed, French landscapes, a view of Amherst, prints of Africa and America, as well as the broadside ballads that Thomas printed and sold by the thousands.

The rear room is where most of the demonstration printing is done. Here is the case of upper- and lower-case Caslon type, the double desk where accounts are kept and orders recorded, a shelf with bottles, jug, tin trunks, and lamp. A small stove, made in the 1830's, heats the room because press inks cannot do a good job at low temperature. The press is an Acorn, named

10 TOMMY THUMB's
Ne, he, he, he.

Moo, Moo, Moo.

Cock,

for the shape of its end piece, made by Smith, Hoe & Company of New York City in the 1820's. Following the Columbia press, made at Philadelphia about 1814, and the Wells press of Hartford, patented in 1819, this press, patented in 1821, was the third iron press made in this country. One may watch the printer ink the press, close the frisket and tympan containing the paper over the type bed, and pull the toggle joint to produce a copy of the Boston and Albany mail-stage notice of 1812, the program of an exhibition at Gilmanton Academy in 1802, or a 1790 issue of the *Massachusetts Spy*. It was not until the perfection of the rotary press and the application of steam power that presses could turn out multiple copies in one smooth operation. All type in the Village Printing Office must be set by hand, the compositor laboriously picking out the characters, spacing words, and punctuating with the use of a composing stick. It is from this type, locked into a form on the press, that the printed page is produced.

While the Printing Office reflects some of Thomas' publishing and book-selling activities, it is by no means a typical large shop. The old screw press in the front room was considerably

The Acorn press.

outmoded by 1830, although it was no doubt still in use in some country areas. The single Acorn press could not have turned out a great deal of work, although it might indeed be the only press in a small shop. This printing office simply attempts to show some of the equipment and methods used by a publisher and job printer of the early nineteenth century. Isaiah Thomas had twelve presses in his Worcester office in the 1790's, five in his Boston office. Besides this he had branches or affiliations in other areas of Massachusetts and in Vermont, New York, and Maryland. In addition to his newspaper he published some 400-odd volumes, among them Webster's *Speller*, Pike's *Arithmetic*, Latin and Greek grammars, Paine's *Age of Reason*, Sterne's *Sentimental Journey*, Richardson's *Pamela*, and Goldsmith's *Vicar of Wakefield*, as well as juvenile titles, including Mother Goose and *Robinson Crusoe*, and his famous Almanac, Bible, and *Worcester Collection of Sacred Harmony*. He gradually lost interest in his business after 1810 but he went on to write a *History of Printing in America* that is still a standard reference and to found in Worcester the American Antiquarian Society, one of the great research libraries in this country.

The old wooden press.

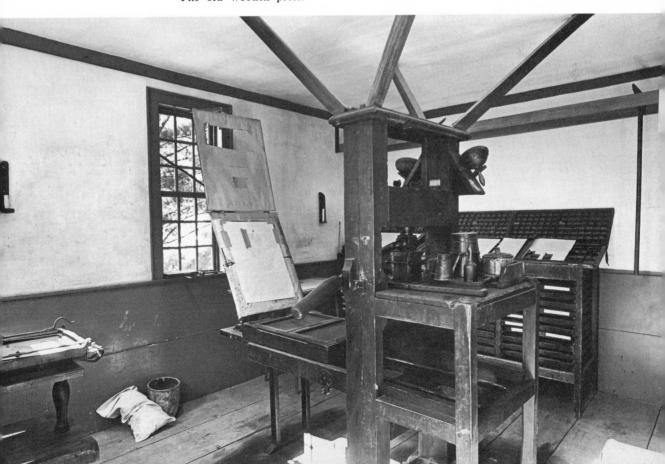

The Blacksmith Shop.

The Shops and Mills 8

The Blacksmith Shop

English settlers of the seventeenth century and their successors in the eighteenth and early nineteenth centuries never were able to manage for long without the services of a blacksmith. Many newly organized towns advertised for blacksmiths, some going so far as to offer land for a house or farm, or some other inducement, to any blacksmith who would settle among them. These craftsmen were needed to shoe horses and oxen, make hardware for the buildings that were going up, make and repair tools and machine parts for farmers and other craftsmen, make and repair kitchen utensils. Occasionally they even engaged in the simple task of making nails. Their ability, like that of every artisan, varied from one craftsman to another. The accounts of some blacksmiths indicate that they were occupied only in shoeing livestock, tiring wheels, repairing toasters and trivets, replacing a cog or a screw, or hammering out a simple hook or trammel. Others engaged in the far more skillful labor of fashioning kettles and frying pans, making delicate machinery parts, turning out ploughs and rakes and harrows. Some few, highly skilled indeed, were able to work with millwrights, inventive mechanics, and mechanical geniuses to make the parts

for the mills, machines, and tools that in the course of the early nineteenth century were to revolutionize the textile industry and to form the basis of a machine-tool industry.

The Blacksmith Shop at the Village comes from Bolton, Massachusetts, a small town in the center of the state. It was built for Moses Wilder some time after 1802. This stone shop had two forges—one evidently for Moses' son, Abraham, who was working with his father in the 1820's. The property was sold by a younger son about the time of the Civil War, at which point it ceased to operate as a blacksmith shop.

The building has well-placed windows, which give the demonstrating blacksmith daylight to work by as well as the light he receives from his fire. The huge bellows fan and control the charcoal fire as the blacksmith hammers out a hook or a handle, roughens out a cart iron for fitting on the wheel, or shapes a rod into nails of whatever length. The original New England blacksmith, if he was to do more, had to be a mechanic of no little ability, and he had to have a working knowledge of engineering and hydraulics as well. His knowledge and ability, hand in hand with the vision of the inventor, helped shape the course of New England's industrial revolution.

The Cabinet Shop

The cabinetmaker in rural New England did not ordinarily work at his trade all year round. He was a farmer first of all, and in his spare time, particularly during the winter months, he made simple pieces of furniture for the local trade. Chairs, tables, beds, cupboards, candlestands, cradles, simple chests of drawers, and desks—this was the extent of his furniture making. As a turner and joiner he also made small woodenware: boxes, dough troughs, meal chests, possibly spinning wheels and reels, stools, bed wrenches, and cheese presses. He might also have done some carpentering and perhaps was called in to make a cornice or an architrave for a room or a door. Some few cabinetmakers plied their trade most of the time, and they usually had help from a journeyman and perhaps an apprentice. Infrequently they were highly skilled craftsmen who turned out fine pieces of furniture that sold outside the community,

sometimes as part of the coastal trade, or sometimes for export
to the West Indies. Only now are we beginning to identify a few
of these country cabinetmakers and to recognize their work.

The Old Sturbridge Village Cabinet Shop is an odd little
structure, built in the late eighteenth century on Village property. Its small windows, high ridgepole, and incongruous front
door are clearly replacements from several sources, but no one
today remembers when and from where. Some years ago it

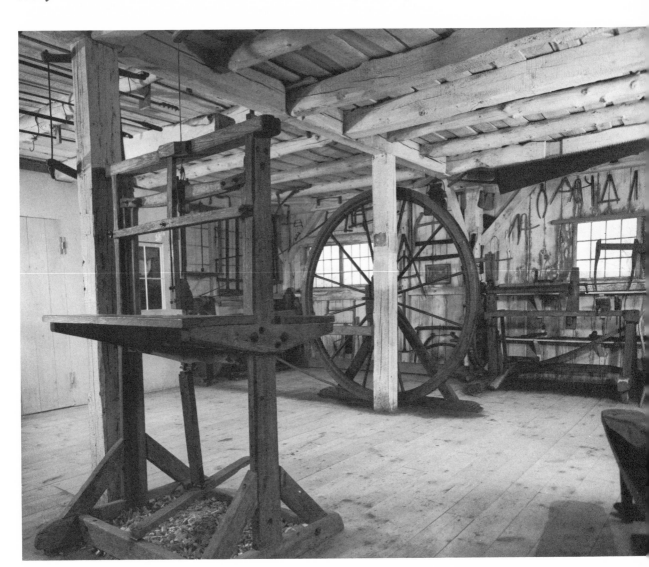

The Cabinet Shop.

looked as though it had come from the Pennsylvania Dutch country, so gay was it in its paint of pink and blue, but it has since faded into the soft gray it is today.

The interior walls are lined with the tools of the cabinet-maker's trade: adzes, saws, hammers, knives, awls, bits and braces, gauges, planes. To one side is a large lathe. An apprentice had to work the wheel while the cabinetmaker turned his bedpost or table leg or chair stretcher. His stains, waxes, and paints are at the rear, as are his lengths and blocks of wood—mainly cherry, maple, pine, and mahogany, with a few others for inlay, for backs of drawers, or for decorative contrast.

The Pewterer's Shop

New England was filled with pewterers in the late eighteenth century, although they began to turn to other trades and other materials as the nineteenth century wore on. Woodenware had been most commonly used on dining tables in the seventeenth century, and its popularity continued in rural communities in the eighteenth. By 1700, however, New England artisans were making their own pewter, and the names of such skilled pewterers as the Boardmans soon became known throughout the region. At the same time pewter was imported from England and to some extent from France. Much of it was melted down to make bullets during the Revolution, and to make other objects afterward. In the course of the nineteenth century the use of pewter gave way to that of porcelain and earthenware, but it was still commonly used in New England homes in 1800 and 1820. Increasingly it was made of a harder alloy known as Britannia ware. Gradually its use died out, and the hundreds of pewterers became workers in copper, brass, iron, silver, or other metals.

In the Old Sturbridge Village Pewterer's Shop the pewterer pours molten pewter into spoon or button molds, and finishes and polishes his pieces. On a shelf running around two sides of the shop are some of the wares New England pewterers made and sold—porringers, teapots, plates, dishes, pans, tankards, mugs, beakers, boxes, lamps, and candlesticks. The demonstrating craftsman has a pot of molten pewter—a mixture of tin,

antimony, and lead—over the fire. He pours the liquid carefully into his molds, lets it cool, loosens it with a quick, precise
blow, and then proceeds to take it out, smooth the edges, and
rub and polish it.

The Tinsmith Shop

The Tinsmith Shop is crowded with a lathe, cutters, trim-
ming and turning tools, pieces of old tinware to be repaired,
patterns for new pieces, and even old crockery and earthenware

The Pewterer's Shop.

The Tinsmith Shop.

pieces brought in for a mending job with tin. A tinsmith could make almost any vessel—coffeepots and teapots, pails measures, lanterns, candlesticks, funnels, candle boxes, oil cans, baking pans, candle molds, milk pans, colanders, powder cannisters, roasters, graters, skimmers, pitchers, needle cases, bread and apple trays, foot stoves, dust pans, snuffers and trays, tea caddies, dredgers—almost anything that was needed. Often he did not decorate his tin unless he had an assistant skilled in this task. More often he sold it plain and left the decorating for others to do. Sometimes whole families eked out their incomes by decorating tinware. Tinplate or sheet tin was imported from England and purchased by tinsmiths. The tinsmith could cut out his sheet to a desired shape, form it with his tools, and solder the parts together. New Englanders, notably the tinsmiths of Berlin and Meriden, Connecticut, peddled their tin up and

The Broommaker Shop.

down the seacoast and even carried it into the new western territories. At least one enterprising tinsmith and japanner of Hartford sold directly to the peddlers and thus avoided having to go on the road himself. By 1830 the tinplate industry, as it was called, was one of the most extensive in New England.

The Broommaker Shop

The little Broommaker Shop is a small, one-room operation that nevertheless turns out an amazing number of brooms each year. With the aid of his broom machine the broommaker can gather, cut, wrap, and fasten his broom, turn his handle, and produce a complete broom in a matter of minutes.

Housewives of the early eighteenth century used bundles

of twigs or splintered wood to sweep their floors, but after the Revolution some farmers in the Connecticut River Valley began experimenting with the growing of broomcorn. Traditionally, Levi Dickinson is credited with growing the first crop in Hadley in the 1790's, but broomcorn was known earlier. The tall stalks in the fall were dried, hetcheled, and carried to the broommaker. By 1830 more than fifty thousand bushels of this corn were raised in the vicinity of Northampton alone. By 1850 close to a million brooms were made annually in New England, after which time western competition ended the industry. New England brooms, like New England tinware, were carried south and west in the peddlers' carts.

The Pottery Shop

Every New England community that had clay nearby had at least a part-time potter—a man who set up his wheel, built his kiln inside or in his yard, built himself a pug mill, and opened for business. He sold his wares to housewives, to the local general stores, to larger markets, or to peddlers. Sometimes he himself went from door to door in his area, or once a year made a peddling trip south. Hundreds of thousands of pieces of New England redware and stoneware were thus turned out and sold locally or at a distance. It was only after the introduction of motor-driven machinery that the potter became a full-time operator, with specialized assistants, who sold largely to wholesalers.

The Hervey Brooks Pottery Shop came to Sturbridge from Goshen, Connecticut. Hervey Brooks built the little shop about 1805, and there he potted for more than sixty years— making redware pans, jugs, jars, porringers, bowls, and an occasional inkstand, churn, or washbowl. After the influx of cheap English wares in the 1830's and 1840's, he made greater quantities of flowerpots and stovepipes. He dug clay from nearby pits, turned and shaped his wares, glazed and decorated them, baked them in his kiln, packed and sold them at retail and wholesale. Many of his sales were to peddlers, who sold his wares as far south as Georgia and westward along the frontier.

On one side of the shop is the Pug Mill, used to break up the large lumps of clay before the clay is further processed for making redware. Usually pug mills were powered by a horse owned or hired by the potter. Inside is a small mill for grinding glazes or pigments used in coloring and decorating pottery. This mill is a reproduction of one owned by Hervey Brooks. In the oval brick kiln, often pronounced "kill," pieces are fired after being shaped. The demonstrating potter is usually at work at his wheel, turning out the same kinds of vessels as Brooks did a century and a half ago. An old redware pie plate with "apple pie" on it in yellow slip, a porringer, a pitcher, or a beanpot can be quickly and easily duplicated by the Village potter, who on days when he is not busy at the wheel, will dip and decorate his wares, let them dry, and carefully stack them in his kiln for baking.

The kiln at the Pottery Shop.

The Cooperage

At the present writing at least one other shop is in the process of erection—a cooperage that is going up on the farm. When completed it will show what was an essential industry to the New Englanders, who had to pack and transport their fish, flour, gunpowder, nails, salted meats, and other products, and who had to store cider, foods, and articles of daily use in barrels and kegs in their own homes.

The Gristmill

New England's industrial predominance in the nineteenth century was made possible in part by its terrain. Its numerous streams and rivers were an easy source of water power in nearly every town, and windmills were almost unknown except in a few areas along the coast. The origins of New England industry go back to its earliest days, when the settlers had to have a gristmill to grind grain, a sawmill to cut trees into boards for buildings, and a fulling mill to process home-woven cloth—to pound the threads close together, shrink it, dye it, and bring up a nap. Milton, Massachusetts, claims the distinction of having the first gristmill; in 1634 it granted Israel Stoughton permission to cut town timber in order to erect it. Often towns voted land, grinding privileges, a percentage of the grain, tax exemptions, and even money to any individual who would erect and operate a gristmill.

The three little mills on the pond at Old Sturbridge Village are a gristmill, carding mill, and sawmill, all close to the site of an early gristmill. Eventually the Village hopes to have a second mill center with additional mills and factories. Most towns by 1800 had two or three mills on each river site with sufficient flow of water, and around the mills grew a village, usually with a meetinghouse, a schoolhouse, and a few stores and shops as well as houses. Sometimes these centers remained separate villages within a township, sometimes they petitioned to be incorporated as separate towns, and sometimes, as the nineteenth century drew to a close, they merged with a second and third village and became a scarcely identifiable section of a large town.

The Village Gristmill is a two-story structure covered with unpainted clapboards. The porch running across its front is a rather unusual feature. The building was not modeled after any specific structure but incorporates the typical features of mills of its period. The machinery came from the Porter Gristmill in Hebron, Connecticut. The wheel in its raceway is a huge wooden overshot wheel.

Inside the mill, along one side are the scales, grain chest, and other appropriate miscellany. At the rear is a long table where the miller sorts and packages his flours. Here are the

The Gristmill.

The grindstones.

bolting cloths that sift the meal into coarse, medium, and fine flour, the barrels and bins tightly secured against dust and damp, the wooden dollies that carry the heavy bags to waiting carts and wagons, and grain scoops and shovels.

On the opposite side are the grindstones, huge stones of French buhr that came into this country in large quantities as ballast in ocean-going vessels. These stones, the top fitting almost but not quite against the bottom, require frequent picking or roughening as the surfaces are worn smooth by the friction of grinding. If they fit too closely, both grain and stones will be damaged. Their fit can be adjusted by turning a screw adjusting the bearing. These stones can grind up to sixty pounds of wheat per hour before the friction makes the flour so hot

Bolting and sifting.

as to cause it to mold after packaging. If it is damp and then hot, it may ferment, and a bag of fermented grain or meal is a most unpleasant object. The grain is poured into the hopper above the stones by the miller, is broken up by them into meal, which contains husks, then falls into a pit from which an endless belt with small buckets carries it to the floor above, where it passes through a series of sifting or bolting cloths and then into a storage bin from which it descends by gravity for bagging. The whole ingeniously mechanized operation, a forerunner of today's automation, was developed by Oliver Evans, an eighteenth-century Pennsylvania inventor. It was in part from the first (1795) and later editions of his *Young Millwright's Guide* that a new mill wheel was built a few years ago and the operation (which had been anachronistically electrical) brought back to period.

New Englanders grew several grains in their fields—wheat, rye, Indian corn, buckwheat, and oats—but their largest cereal crop was Indian corn. This is the meal that most farm families cooked and ate in the form of cornmeal mush, corn bread, Indian pudding, or johnnycake. Mixed with rye, it made a New England farm bread known as Indian or ryeninjun, which is baked today in the Village farm kitchen. The grain could be pounded at home with mortar and pestle, a laborious and unsatisfactory job, or it could be taken by the bushel to the local gristmill for grinding. Sometimes the housewife did her own sieving to produce flour from meal, but as the nineteenth century advanced she was more and more willing to leave that task to the capable hands of the miller and his machinery. By the mid-eighteenth century there were usually several gristmills in each of the larger towns and they did not even begin to be superseded until the opening of the Erie Canal made it possible after 1825 to import Western wheat. Even so, a few New England gristmills are still grinding with stones to produce the stone-ground flours preferred by fine bakers and discriminating diners today.

The Sawmill

The Village Sawmill unfortunately is not an operating mill. Its machinery is from the Old Cheney Mill in Gilead, Connecticut, but it has never been put in working order since its removal. The building itself, like the Gristmill, is a rough approximation of an early mill. The saw is an up-and-down type, successor to the older and primitive pit saw, which was operated by two men standing in a pit under it. The up-and-down saw made parallel marks in boards, easily distinguishable from marks made by a circular saw or band saw, which were later developments. Some circular saws were in use in the Village period, but they were not widespread. The carriage that holds the log is in place in this mill, as is the raceway leading to the mill from the pond. The Village has plans for putting into operation either this or another sawmill at some future time.

The high cost of transporting lumber overland caused towns
and villages to set up mills for cutting construction boards.
Where logs could be floated downriver the problem was simple,
but this was possible only when streams were high and free
of ice. Thus, so long as there was timber to be cut there were
small local mills, quite aside from the large operations in the
timber country of the northern states. It was not until the ad-
vent of steam power and the disappearance of timber on most
farm lands that the small local mills began to close. Cheap
transportation and the expense of putting in power-operated
equipment hastened their departure, but a few were still in
existence at the close of the nineteenth century.

The Sawmill.

The Carding Mill

The Carding Mill was originally built in South Waterford, Maine, probably in the 1830's. It evidently replaced a mill that had been on the property prior to 1819. Oliver Hapgood, who had migrated from Sutton, Massachusetts, built the first and probably the second mill. In the 1830's it contained one carding machine and several pickers. Later another carding machine was added.

The mill was brought to the Village as the gift of the late Albert W. Rice. It was re-erected, a raceway built, and a flutter or tub wheel installed, and it will shortly open to the public looking much as it did in South Waterford. It will contain an opener, a picker, and a finishing machine that makes the rolls.

Carding machines began appearing in New England around the year 1790. They were first perfected in England and the knowledge of how to make them smuggled into this country by workers from English factories. Prior to that time all carding was done by hand, usually in the home. The wool when it came from the fleece had to be washed, picked over for bits of dirt, burrs, twigs, and other foreign matter, and have a little oil added. It was then carefully combed or carded on hand cards, which resemble the stiff, rectangular wire brushes used in combing long-haired dogs today. (These wooden cards had leather faces punctuated with rows of wire teeth. By the time of the Revolution they were being made in New England shops, and many farm families supplemented their incomes by setting teeth into the cards.) The carder first opened, secondly drew together the fibres, and then rolled the combed wool from one card to the other, forming a roll, at which point it was ready for spinning. In 1800 nearly every household spun and wove at least some of its own fabrics, and machines that would take over this slow, laborious work were a great boon to the textile maker. John and Arthur Scholfield of Connecticut and Massachusetts, two of the English immigrants who brought their mechanical secrets with them, made the early machines for many shops in these states, and indeed the Village has in one of its buildings, still turning out rolls, a machine of their manufacture that was found in an old barn near Lancaster, New Hampshire. They built one of their earliest machines at Montville, Connecticut, where they charged seven cents per pound for "picking, breaking, and carding wool," nine cents when oil had to be added; then they moved on to Pittsfield, where they manufactured machines for sale. A Litchfield operator in 1803 assured housewives:

The wool by running through the machine becomes thoroughly mixed, the rolls are even and clear of knots, and a woman will spin one-third more for a day's task from these rolls than from those which are carded by hand. The yarn runs more fine and even; the cloth dresses free from cockles, and of course is more handsome and durable. Rolls thus manufactured may be carried in a wrapper any distance without injury.

One operator in Burlington, Connecticut, refused to accept wool with oil in it, preferring to add the lanolin himself. He specialized in carding merino wool, for which there was an enormous demand during and immediately following the War

The Carding Mill.

of 1812. By 1810 there were more than seven hundred machines operating in small mills in New England, and this number was to increase in the years before 1830. According to Barnes Riznik, Director of Museum Interpretation at Old Sturbridge Village, who has thoroughly investigated the subject,

Early machines in the Carding Mill.

there were more than forty separately identifiable New England shops making carding machines before 1840.

Of these three small mills—the Gristmill, Sawmill, and Carding Mill—only the Carding Mill reflects the beginnings of New England's industrial revolution. The others, with minor revision, could as easily have operated in the early eighteenth century as in the early nineteenth. But the machines in the Carding Mill, crude and rudimentary as they are, represent an inventive ingenuity and a technological advance in use of materials and elimination of hand labor. They were the harbingers of the steam-powered, large-scale industrial machines that were to appear after 1825 up and down the New England countryside. Old Sturbridge Village in time will carry New England's industrial story a bit further, will have a cotton-weaving factory or a spinning factory, or perhaps the two combined, and will develop other factories and mills representative of the second stage of the region's industrial expansion.

The John Fenno House.

The Residences   9

The first European settlers in New England lived in hastily dug out cellars, in simple one- or two-room structures, or in community shelters. When they began erecting houses they modeled them after what they had known back in England, simple rectangles, often with overhangs, infrequently half-timbered. These houses often began as single-room dwellings, to which were later added a lean-to, other rooms, and a second story.

In the early eighteenth century the colonists began copying the formal, classical design of English Georgian architecture. Sometimes the houses were square, with a chimney at either end and with four rooms, two on either side of a central hall, upstairs and down. Decorative paneling, cornices, architraves, and pediments decorated the interior, and sometimes there were columns at the front entrance. After the Revolution this style was modified as a lighter, more delicate-appearing decoration was used. This new Federal style in turn gave way after 1825 to Greek Revival architecture, where the inspiration was the classical remains of ancient Greece rather than Rome. The traditional Greek temple with portico, columns, and side entrance became the most popular house style. Side by side with this development was the purely institutional architecture of the factory and mill, the shop and the retail store.

The residences around the Village Green were all built be-

tween 1704 and 1796: the John Fenno House in 1704, the
Stephen Fitch House in 1737, the Solomon Richardson House
about 1748, and the Salem Towne House in 1796. Two of
them are late seventeenth and early eighteenth century in style,
one Georgian (the Richardson House), and one Federal (the
Salem Towne House). None is Greek Revival in style. All
these styles were still extant and the houses in practical use in
1820 and 1830. All are on the Village Green, furnished as the
homes of gentlemen and men of a profession or as the homes
of farmers and artisans; features of the early eighteenth century can be seen side by side with those of the early nineteenth
—featheredge sheathing of 1700 and outside shutters of 1800.

All four houses are furnished as they would have been by
1820 or 1830, still with the cherished or just plain old, shabby,
and old-fashioned in use in nearly every room, with many
pieces purchased at the time of setting up housekeeping in 1780
or 1800, and with a few possessions long coveted, saved for,
finally acquired, and proudly displayed in the parlors and dining
areas. Thus a beautifully made gate-leg table and a hanging
shelf of the early eighteenth century are relegated to upstairs
chambers, a fine early chest is in a shed ell, and a courting
mirror hangs behind a door, while eagle-decorated Hitchcock
chairs, painted floor cloths, Empire sofas, and heavy pedestal
tables occupy places of honor in parlors and dining rooms. The
connoisseur of fine early furniture and decorative pieces may
throw up his hands in despair, but Horace Mann and Nailer
Tom and the Reverend William Ellery Channing would have
felt quite at home in these surroundings.

The families who lived in these houses were all village-born
and bred. None was an immigrant, and few ventured far from
town except to market or on a rare visit to relatives at a distance. Most of them had never been to Boston, less than seventy
miles to the east, and many had never even visited the county
seat in Worcester. Only Salem Towne and his family had spent
time in Boston, and only the attorney, John McClellan, had
been in Hartford and in the nation's capital, Washington.
Among them he alone had traveled to Pennsylvania and Georgia, to western New York State and Ohio, but had returned to
reside in a country town.

Isolated and insular as they were, these families lived closely together. Busy housewives could still take time to run in to help a neighbor who was ill, care for a newborn baby until his mother was strong enough to do so, sit through the night at the bedside of the dying, or care for the young children of a newly bereaved farmer. This kind of neighborly assistance they took for granted, just as they took it for granted that they themselves would have help when it was time to quilt a coverlet, make up the funeral garb when death had visited them, or prepare for a wedding celebration. The men could count on help at harvesting, when stones or trees had to be pulled from a field, and at cider-making time. Mrs. Towne had help in the house, but farm women had only their own daughters and part-time hired girls, all the daughters of neighbors.

The daily routine of living was the same in all these houses. People were early risers in an age before electricity made late hours practical. They rose before dawn in winter, with the sun in summer, and their hours were filled until the curfew hour of nine in the evening. Women cooked and baked, made cheeses and butter, fed their families, made the clothing and most of the bed and table linens, scrubbed and laundered, beat carpets and sanded floors, made soap and candles, spun and wove and sewed, all without much thought for the rigors of their lot. Such labor was universal, and if Mrs. Towne, as a woman of position in town, did not do a great deal of the housework herself, she supervised those who did, and on her rested the responsibility for the training of her children. These houses were crowded with children. If a woman had few of her own, there were always relatives' children, orphaned or just staying with her while attending school. There was little privacy in these small houses—having a room to oneself was a luxury unheard of in childhood, seldom known even by adults. It was unsatisfactory in any case, for in the rigorous New England winters people were glad to sleep two or more to a bed.

The parlors of farmers' and artisans' homes were little used. They were reserved for important occasions—for funerals, visits by the minister, Thanksgiving celebrations. Most family living was done in the kitchen, particularly in winter, and around the fireplace. If the house had a sitting room, this was used when there were guests, for ordinary parties, for quilting bees and teas. Bedchambers, unheated except in time of illness, were reserved for sleeping only. The Towne House and that of the attorney perhaps were exceptions. The Townes used their parlor for normal entertaining, they often ate in the dining room, and Mrs. Towne occasionally did her mending in her bedroom. The children also played in their rooms on rainy days, but even in this house the ordinary family gathering places were the kitchen and the sitting room opposite. There was no formal living in the ordinary New England village, although there were some pretensions to copying the manners and customs of polite society in the larger towns. Thus when Mrs. Towne entertained, she used silver and porcelain, often served an evening supper, and ordered some of her delicacies from Boston. Farmers and artisans entertained in their kitchens at dinner or tea, or in their sitting rooms.

The task of re-erecting, working out interior and exterior details, and furnishing the Village residences, as indeed all the exhibition buildings, has required the combined efforts of the entire Village staff, although chief responsibility lies with the curatorial department. The maintenance department, under exacting supervision, erects, plasters, and paints the buildings. The curatorial department furnishes them, often with advice and assistance from research, from the conservator, from the garden committee, and from the craft-demonstrations department.

The decision to acquire a building is based on the need for that particular structure to help tell the Village story, its availability and condition, and the ease with which it can be moved. Unless small enough to be moved intact or in sections, it must be taken down board by board, every piece carefully marked, and reconstructed slowly and painstakingly with the aid of numerous photographs. Meanwhile the research department searches the land records, town records, and any other source bearing on its history, the curator of architecture makes a careful architectural record and supervises every detail of reconstruction, the conservator is called in when puzzling elements or inconsistencies can be checked in his laboratory, and the curatorial staff is busy collecting furniture, china, kitchen and fireplace utensils, linens, pictures, and the like, supervises the making of curtains, upholstering of chairs and sofas, weaving

of carpets, and restoration of coverlets; orders custom-made
curtain rods, nails for hanging, and other necessary hardware;
and sees to the repair or restoration of a chandelier, a firescreen,
a chest covered with layers of paint, or a stained and fly-specked
print.

Essential to the furnishings of the residences is a sure knowledge of the decorative arts, the history of New England, and
the social picture of the early nineteenth century. The evidence
may be found in diaries, journals, and letters, in newspaper
accounts and advertisements, in paintings, engravings, and
prints, in account books, ledgers, and bills of sale, in all the
sources that bit by bit add up to a picture of the exterior and
interior of a rural house and the activities of its occupants. The
long chain of history in this case must work horizontally, cutting across from what was in one house, one diary, one newspaper advertisement, to the accumulated evidence of several
sources and then to what will go into a residence in the Village.
The research is endless, but the affection for and pride in an
authentically furnished house is the reward.

Thus the blue-checked curtains in the Fitch House summer
kitchen are documented by the inventory of the possessions
John McClellan took from his father's house after the old gentleman's death in 1807, by fragments of curtains and hangings
in museums, by several rural inventories, and by a traveler's
comment when he visited Durham, Connecticut, in 1792. Those
in the Richardson House parlor are copied from an old hanging
in the possession of the Society for the Preservation of New
England Antiquities; the hanging came from a house in Old
Lyme, Connecticut, and appears to have been made for the
windows there sometime between 1790 and 1810. The curtains
in the Towne House parlor and dining room are from a penciled
sketch, and those in the Farmhouse parlor from a Connecticut
portrait. A newspaper advertisement in Portsmouth in 1816
listed in an auction sale a "canary cage and bowl for gold and
silver fish," which must have been like the multipurpose object
in the Towne House parlor.

The absence of curtains and carpets in all but the principal
rooms of the more humble dwellings in the Village is documented by many diaries and journals of the period. The "several cheap prints" of the "Prodigal Son . . . The Industrious

Apprentice . . . Sheepshearing, a Farmyard, and a Harvest Scene," which served as "Amusement to the Children" and might provide a moral lesson in Enos Hitchcock's *Farmers Friend*, published in 1793, are seen in the parlors of the Towne House and Richardson House. Harriet Martineau noted that she was heartily tired of seeing such prints in nearly every New England tavern she stayed at in the 1830's. Roger Minot Sherman of Fairfield, Connecticut, purchased in 1816 a floor cloth like that in the Towne House; Harriet Beecher Stowe's mother made one, as did countless other New England housewives. There are many advertisement and inventory records for the Scotch Ingrain carpets in the Fenno House east chamber and the Towne House sitting room.

But the effort that goes into a house restoration does not stop at what is authentic for the period. It must also consider the family that presumably lived in the house, the number of people and their ages and sex, their social position, their occupations, and the intricacies of their personalities. In the case of the Village residences we have substantial knowledge of only one family, the Salem Townes. We know very little about John Fenno, Stephen Fitch, and Solomon Richardson, and in any case by 1830 or so their houses would have been altered by their descendants. Thus it has taken more creative imagination to furnish these houses than the Towne House.

Only one, the Fenno House, is unpainted, because by the third decade of the nineteenth century the majority of New England houses were painted, even in rural areas. All have gardens and flower beds, as did all country houses where there was time to spare. The fences, the woodpiles, the wells and sheds and barns are authentic surroundings, though their appearance is perhaps a bit too neat for what we know were often untidy, cluttered dooryards and commons of their day. The grass is cut a little short to accommodate modern visitors; an attempt is made to restrain the fly and rodent population that overran New England villages; and for their own safety as well as that of visitors, the geese, sheep, and cattle are not allowed to roam at large. Otherwise the staff has created as closely to the original as possible the appearance and the aura of rural New England in the early nineteenth century.

The John Fenno House

The John Fenno House fronts the Village Green below and to one side of the Meetinghouse, beyond the Herb Barn and Garden. It seems somehow to stand apart, secret, wrapped in reminiscences of the early eighteenth century. It was built in Canton, Massachusetts, a small town south of Boston, in the year 1704. John Fenno was a yeoman whose father had purchased the old Roger Clapp property (in what was then Stoughton), which had formerly belonged to the Ponkapaug Indian tribe. John, who was born in nearby Milton in 1665, married a girl from Braintree (now Quincy), who bore him nine children. Obviously he needed a house of some size for this family, and ten years after the birth of his eldest son, Isaac, he built this two-story structure, a rarity for its day.

Fenno was a man of some independence of mind and perhaps quarrelsome. Brought before the church for agreeing to engage in a duel, he challenged the belief that dueling was sinful but complied with the church's demand that he make a public confession. He was later tried for perjury and was acquitted. His lifetime spanned two centuries. His father had fought in King Philip's War and two of his grandsons were soldiers of the Revolution. He was a farmer of moderate means; the inventory of his estate taken after his death put a value of only about $5,000 on his household goods, farm stock, and real estate.

The Fenno House, known in Canton as the "red house," which must once have been its color, is a central-chimney structure with entry and staircase in front of the chimney and with a room on either side upstairs and down. A small shed extension at the rear of the kitchen gives additional space. Seen from outside, the front appears asymmetrical, since there is only one window on one side of the door, two on the other. The clapboard exterior today is unpainted.

The house is furnished as it would have been after a century and a quarter of existence, with much that was old in 1830 and some of what was new, the household goods of a farmer-artisan in a rural community. If one enters through the front entry, or porch as it was known in the seventeenth century, he will find the kitchen on his left. Dominant in this room is the great fireplace with beehive oven that reaches toward the second story. One can imagine the meals that were served from this kitchen, the pot of beans baked on Saturday for the Sabbath when no cooking might be done, the loaves of bread, the pies, stews, custards, Indian puddings, soups, and "made dishes" (casseroles). One gets the impression from contemporary writers that the kitchen was what we today would call the family room, where all the household gathered for meals, for sitting about the fire in the evening, for most family activities when company was not present. The corner shelves look as though knocked together by a teen-age son at his mother's behest. Those over

Fenno House parlor.

the fireplace must have been made to order for the absent-minded cook who no sooner had her soup put together and simmering when she realized she had forgotten salt. Such necessities could be lined up on the shelves for the would-be well-organized housewife.

One of the finest pieces in this room is the hutch table, that eighteenth-century equivalent of today's convertible furniture. At the turn of a wrist it can become a small settle, or the back can be let down to form a table top. The illusion of space in a museum display is deceptive; these early kitchens were crowded with all the paraphernalia of living, and versatile furniture was a boon to the housewife. The rear door opens into a long shed where stores of flour, sugar, molasses, apples, cheeses,

Fenno House kitchen.

Fenno House west chamber.

and salt meats were kept, where much household gear was stored, and where the unwary visitor might trip over the wash-tub or board, the baby walker, or the warping frames.

Opposite the kitchen is the parlor, with whitewashed walls, paneled fireplace walls, and five windows. The woodwork here is painted a gray-blue, a color not original to this room though found on woodwork in an upstairs chamber. The fireplace wall is covered with featheredged sheathing, and the fireplace itself is enclosed in a simple frame without shelf. The maple gate-leg table in the center, large enough to accommodate a game, a family reading of verse or novel, or a musical group when there were visitors, has on it the family Bible. Chippendale ladder-back chairs, a Windsor rocker, and a country wing chair grace the home-woven carpet. The walls are adorned with a Chippendale looking glass, a map of the northern United States by John Melish dated 1816, a paper cut-out, portraits of D. F. Newell by Francis Alexander and of a Mr. Gifford of Cranston, Rhode Island, an 1832 reprint of Paul Revere's famous engraving of the Boston Massacre, and silhouettes that might have been cut by an itinerant profile maker or by a self-taught member of the household. The desk-on-frame against the rear wall is a mid-eighteenth-century piece. The cupboard at the side of the fire-

Shed at the Fenno House.

place contains tea equipage and a few ornaments, and a copper kettle stands on the hearth.

The narrow staircase turns sharply as it ascends to the second story. Here the east chamber is comfortably furnished with a low post bed, fine William and Mary highboy, small table, tape loom and chair, and Sheraton mahogany chest of drawers. A framed 1702 print of Cotton Mather's map of New England and a fine pastel portrait hang on the walls. The sheathing on the fireplace wall, like the rest of the woodwork in the upstairs chambers, is unpainted.

The west chamber is fitted out as a man's and boy's bedroom plus storeroom. The fine trestle-foot gate-leg table descends from the early eighteenth century, and the painted chest, probably of Connecticut Valley origin, is decorated with tree, circle, and other designs. Two other chests, one with painted graining, and a third with applied spindles, serve as closets. The chairs are early Carver armchairs, relics of a day before this house was built.

Outside, the sheltering tree in front, the fence and hitching post, the well-tended kitchen garden at the side, and the vegetable garden sloping down at the rear set off this simple Massachusetts farmhouse which had adapted gradually and gracefully to the demands of the early nineteenth century.

The Fitch House

The Stephen Fitch House, the first residence brought into the Village, was erected in Windham, Connecticut, in 1735–37 on a piece of land that is now part of the town of Willimantic. Miss Helen G. Holley, retired director of host and hostesses at Old Sturbridge Village, has done much research on this house

The Fitch House.

Fitch House kitchen door.

161

and its owners and believes that Stephen Fitch followed a family tradition when he purchased this tract from among the finest land in Windham. He was descended from a family that had served the Colony of Connecticut well and honorably, one of his relatives attaining the rank of governor in the years prior to the Revolution. In 1737 he married Eleanor Strong of Coventry, by whom he had three sons. He was a farmer but evidently not very successful, or perhaps he invested unwisely or suffered financial setback during the Revolution, for he died insolvent in 1806. Two of his sons seem to have quarreled bitterly over the estate, which a fellow townsman purchased and immediately resold to Jesse, one of the sons. On Jesse's death two years later his brother Stephen purchased the property for somewhat more than the mortgage he held on it, nearly $1,500. Stephen's son, Erastus, operated the house as a tavern for a few years, and it remained in the Fitch family until after the beginning of the twentieth century. The Village purchased it and re-erected it on the Green in 1939.

The house seems to have been built in three stages. The present east parlor was undoubtedly the original single room, as can be realized when one notes the two gun-stock corner posts and the vertical featheredged board sheathing. The west parlor, kitchen, and chamber were probably added about the time of the Revolution, evidently to accommodate a larger family. The ell or summer kitchen at the rear was attached after 1800, probably when Erastus was licensed to keep the house as a tavern.

The building had never been painted before it was removed to Old Sturbridge Village, but today in its tan coat, with its fencing and garden, it is among the most pleasing structures on the Green. One has only to approach it in the early morning when the dew is still heavy to be aware of the charm of the roof line, a half gambrel in front, the solid strength of its front door, the clarity of its line. The overhanging trees, the color in the garden, and the shadow thrown by the well recently acquired in the town of Sturbridge add to the beauty of its exterior.

The east parlor or sitting room was the family gathering room. Here the walnut gate-leg table, finely carved Hadley chest, black-painted rectangular table with elaborately cut apron, fiddle-back chairs, tavern tables, and pine desk no doubt all saw hard use. The books and child's tea set in the cupboard, the baby's cradle, and the toy furniture remind us that children were admitted to this room as a matter of course, as they were excluded from the parlor opposite on all but the most extraordinary occasions. The two oil portraits on the wall, artist unknown, are probably of John and Elizabeth Avery of Stonington, Connecticut. According to tradition, John was a soldier in the Revolution. A pastel portrait of a child by Margaret B.

East parlor in the Fitch House.

Doyle and a register of the Blood family of Pepperell complete the wall decoration.

The west parlor, built in the second half of the eighteenth century, has plastered walls, a dado, and a chimney breast; the mantel evidently was added early in the nineteenth century. This room also has a built-in cupboard. The mahogany shelf clock is by Bishop and Bradley of Watertown, Connecticut, one of the early nineteenth-century clock-making centers, and bears on its glass panel a medallion of Lafayette, beloved of New Englanders. The Empire sofa with horsehair upholstery, extremely popular in the first decades of the nineteenth century, the cherry dropleaf table, the Hitchcock-type chairs with painted eagle decorations, the square inlaid table, and the gilt looking glass would have been cherished pieces reserved for parlor use. The sofa would have been a very recent purchase. On the walls hang portraits of Mr. and Mrs. Southworth Allen Howland of Worcester, a publisher and his writer-editor wife, and a needle-work record of the Thomas Pierce family. The table in the center, used for dining only when the room was opened for guests and holiday entertaining, is a Queen Anne walnut drop-leaf from Mansfield, Connecticut.

Beyond the west parlor is the downstairs chamber, with bright rose-painted walls and white woodwork. The red-painted field bed with its woven coverlet was a fairly new purchase in the early nineteenth century. The Sheraton inlaid chest made of cherry, the red-and-black painted chest on the kitchen wall, and the bandboxes are the only storage receptacles in the room. A courting mirror in its original box, product of the China trade, hangs over one chest.

The chamber door opens into the long red kitchen. Its fire-place, like that of the two parlors, opens into the great central chimney. In or near the fireplace are all the utensils and vessels of cookery—the wrought-iron toaster and trivets, the reflector oven, the wafer iron, the kettles and pots and baking pans, the fry-pans and oven peel and the long-handled ladle. The table is set for family dining with pewter, wood, and earthenware vessels. Farm housewives generally did not use tablecloths for everyday family meals. The dresser on the sitting-room wall holds on its long shelves the crockery, pewter, and tinware used in this household—pans and jugs, cups and pie plates, plates, basins, and teapots. Often the tinware could be purchased from a peddler, while the local potter probably traveled from door to door himself or retailed his wares in the general stores. The worktable near the fireplace, like those in the Fenno and Richardson houses, is where most food preparing was done.

The summer kitchen at the rear houses the Village candlemaking demonstration. Craftswomen in this pleasant, gray-painted room explain to visitors how candles were made by dipping wicking into hot wax or by pouring the wax into molds. Candle molds, deep kettles, pails, skimmers, dippers, candle

Fitch House kitchen.

165

wicking, ladles, stirrers, and shears make up the equipment of this room. A slant cupboard at one end holds kitchen equipment, and beside it is a storage chest. A gray-painted dry sink stands between the two windows on a side wall.

Outside, the kitchen garden basks in the late afternoon sun, as does a tortoise-shell kitten stretched out on the front doorstep. Soon the evening will grow cool, the kitten will depart in search of food and shelter, and the garden will be left to the chipmunks and skunks and woodchucks.

Candle-dipping in the Fitch House summer kitchen.

The Richardson House

The Richardson House was built in Podunk, a section of East Brookfield, Massachusetts, about the year 1748 for one Solomon Richardson. It was moved to Old Sturbridge Village and re-erected in 1940. The building is a New England saltbox, with a long, sloping rear roof, five windows across the front, and

The Richardson House.

center entry. There is a room on either side of the central chimney, upstairs and down, and a long bedroom created by the rear roof line. The exterior is clapboard painted red. The front doorway is somewhat elaborate for a house of this type, with side pilasters and lights and dentiling over the door.

At the time the house was brought to the Village, the founders were not yet insisting on authentic restoration in every detail. They installed in the kitchen their version of a seventeenth-century Essex County fireplace and exposed ceiling joists. These details could not have been in the house originally, but since it was little more than a shell when the Village acquired it, little damage was done. Recently the house has been restored as accurately as could be when many questions had to remain unanswered.

The house nevertheless is representative of many still lived in by New Englanders of the early nineteenth century. The entry walls have a soft colored paper of the period. The parlor is a typical mixture of the old and the new in 1840—old Queen Anne and Chippendale chairs with reproduction "work't seats," a fine old cane-seat chair, and japanned looking glass, new prints of the continents and of cottage scenes and an oil portrait on the walls, a homely carpet woven on a household loom, a country sofa with damask upholstery, a fiddle and stand, and part of an export tea set on a Pembroke table. The dimity curtains are draped with sophistication, revealing that their maker kept abreast of fashion. The room was originally painted the shade of blue on the fireplace paneling.

The sitting room, on the opposite side of the house, is furnished with an eye to easy family living with tables and Windsor chairs for company dining, an oil painting of Franklin flying his famous kite, English Staffordshire and export porcelain in the corner cupboard, and a comfortable wing chair set close to the fire. The fortunate head of this household was the keeper of the town's social library, which his wife required to be housed not in her parlor but in the sitting room, where it would not matter so much if the muddy boots and dusty clothing of borrowers brushed against fabric and furniture.

The kitchen in this house is large enough to accommodate a pull-down bed at one end. The shelves hold a well-polished pewter, pottery, and woodenware. The table near the fireplace

Richardson House parlor.

is the only equivalent of the counter tops of today's functional kitchen. Here, or on the cleared dining table, all mixing, kneading, stirring, and preparing was done. Windsor chairs are set back against the walls or close to the table to give more room, while at the far end, near the bed, yarn winders and a wool wheel remind us that spinning was a routine task in every rural household.

The west chamber upstairs boasts a field bed resplendent in white canopy with netted fringe and candlewick coverlet. Occasionally a weary visitor, footsore after hours of touring, must long to stretch out on its straw-filled mattress. The painted washstand has on it a banded creamware pitcher and bowl, and the dressing table is a concession to leisure and a sense of the amenities. The east chamber, with stenciled walls copied from a fragment found in the house, is a do-it-yourself decorator's dream. The low post bed, Sheraton chest, and square candlestand are painted to resemble wood graining. Most startling is the candlestand, striped in an imitation lignum vitae; not far behind it in appearance is the tiger-maple-grained chest. The long attic room over the kitchen is a bedroom at one end and storage space at the other. Visitors are amused at the full-sized cradle, made not for a baby Amazon but for a bedridden adult.

West chamber of the Richardson House.

One cannot fail to get an impression of greater affluence,
greater interest in style and in the arts in this house than one
gains in the Fenno and Fitch houses. It might perhaps be the
home of a lawyer, the local clergyman, or even of a physician.
The violin, the contemporary prints, the beautifully upholstered
sofa, the elegantly curtained bed, the window curtains, and the
social library all reflect taste and sophistication, an air of world-
liness and of creature comforts. No mere artisan or farmer
would have furnished his home as this is furnished, nor would
he have volunteered his time to service the local library, or had
a tea set in both his parlor and sitting room. Even the flower
beds near the front door and the dazzlingly painted picket fence
hint of a family with some claim to gentility.

The Salem Towne House

When General Salem Towne built his mansion in Charlton,
Massachusetts, in 1796, he chose a site at a crossroad in the
center of town, on a slight rise overlooking the center. His
builder-architect steeped himself in the work of the English
architectural writer William Pain and then erected for him a
handsome country Federal home with white-painted clapboard
exterior, green shutters, monitor roof, and handsome fan-
lighted doorway. The house is square with entrances on all
four sides; a central hall runs down its length, and there are
two rooms and chimney on either side. The attached barn,
sheds, and the ell at rear are modern additions replacing de-
stroyed and burned-out originals.

The house was taken down board by board, stone by stone,
and moved to the Village in 1952–53. There it was carefully
reassembled, restored, furnished, and opened in 1957 as the gift
of Joel Cheney Wells and his wife, Marion Hengerer Wells.

The two rooms on either side of the front doorway, the parlor
and the dining room, have elaborate if "countrified" detail:
parlor chimney piece with pediment, frieze, and urn; door and
window architraves, window seats in the dining room, fine
dentiling, molding, and other detail. Behind the dining room,
separated from it by a small closet with pass-through, is the
kitchen and working fireplace, and behind the parlor is the

sitting room, which the first Salem Towne used as his office. A lower, or summer, kitchen is under the main kitchen. Upstairs, where one might expect to see the same floor plan, there is instead a single room running across the front of the house, with a chamber behind it on either side. This long room, which can be made into two by the simple expedient of drawing together the sliding doors partitioning it off at one end, was intended originally not as a ballroom but as a Masonic meeting room.

The house has been furnished as that of a country magnate

The Salem Towne House.

of some social position but of somewhat uneducated taste and
no great sophistication. The parlor has a fine Federal sofa,
shield-back chairs, a London-made pianoforte, elaborately
carved and gilded looking glass, mahogany secretary with inlaid Masonic symbols, tea table, card table, firescreen, and
needlepoint carpet. The smaller furnishings, the Caughley porcelain tea set, the basket, the child's tea set, books, fans, and
vases reveal that this was a favorite family gathering place, not
just a showpiece set aside for the entertainment of important
visitors.

Towne House parlor.

Salem Towne, Jr., portrait by Francis Alexander.

The dining room, in addition to the usual table and chairs, has a sideboard and a corner mixing table. The punch bowl and glasses, English earthenware, silver, and other appointments reflect the hospitality extended by the family. A portrait of Salem Towne, Jr., painted by Francis Alexander, hangs over the mantel.

Towne House sitting room with portrait of Salem Towne, Sr.

The sitting room behind the parlor was the everyday gathering place, while the desk, maps, surveying instruments, microscope, and books show that it was also Salem Towne's business office. The daybed, toilet articles, invalid's chair, and crutches are evidence of his invalidism in later life. His portrait hangs over the mantel.

The kitchen is crowded with the everyday cooking and house-keeping gear of this family: worktable and chairs, stone sink, shelves filled with crockery and glass; closet holding bottles, jugs, boxes, pots and pans, baking dishes, bins, dough box, all the utensils and tools needed for cooking and serving. Much of the cooking equipment is right on the hearth. No doubt many family meals were eaten here, and it is through this room one passed in entering the house from the sheds. In the lower kitchen, furnished with additional cooking and laundry equipment, there is usually a cooking demonstration—wafer and pie baking, preserving, butter making, and the like.

The lower hall is lined with portraits. From it the stairs rise

Well room in the Towne House.

Towne House ballroom, with All-Seeing Eye.

to a landing lighted by a window that gives a fine view of the quiet pond below. Here hangs one of the finest portraits in the Village collections, John Brewster's painting of his parents.

On the second floor the Masonic meeting room extends across the front of the house. When the Village acquired the building, this room still had some of the original painting on its walls—an overall pattern of trees, probably cedars of Lebanon; these have been retained and restored where necessary. The All-Seeing Eye that was once on the ceiling has been replaced, as have the stars and crescent. Over the mantel are ritual Masonic candlesticks, on the hearth a Masonic brazier, and at one end a Masonic master's chair. A mahogany chamber organ made by Ebenezer Goodrich of Boston stands here. The room is believed to have been partitioned about the year 1807, when the Fayette

Towne House ballroom.

Lodge of Freemasons ceased to meet in the Towne House, possibly because Salem Towne needed the space for his son's growing family; one end is furnished as a bedroom for young boys, with beds, chairs, chests, and all the accumulated toys, games, and other equipment dear to childhood.

Behind the Masonic meeting room on the southwest side is the parents' bedroom, with a high post bed, baby's crib, bureau, serving table, and washstand. On the other side is the chamber used by the girls of the family. The transparent shades at the windows are painted cloth, the carpet home woven, the beds covered with fine chintz, and the toys, school equipment, and toilet array those popular with big and little young ladies of the day.

Salem Towne, who was born in Oxford, Massachusetts, from

Girls' chamber in the Towne House.

which Charlton was later set off, in 1746, was the grandson of the minister of Oxford. His father died while serving in Canada during the Seven Years' War, when Salem was still young, and the fatherless boy achieved his position through his own efforts. His first wife died in childbirth, his second gave him seven children but only one son, and his third, married shortly before he built this house, was never fully accepted by her stepchildren. Perhaps there was some jealousy because Sabra Comans brought several young children of her own to this already crowded household.

Taking an early interest in town affairs, Salem Towne worked himself up in office from dog warden to selectman to representative in the State General Court to member of the

Parents' chamber in the Towne House.

General Court to member of the Governor's Council. He also served in the Massachusetts State Militia during and after the Revolution, retiring with the rank of brigadier general. He was a member of the convention that ratified the new state constitution in 1780. He gradually acquired money and land to add to the social position he had inherited and by 1796 was in a position to build this residence.

His son, Salem, Jr., brought his young wife home after his marriage in 1804 and reared eleven children in the house. He too was a leading townsman, serving in the state militia and legislature and active in the church. He was a member of the Worcester County Agricultural Society and interested in the temperance movement, railroad and turnpike development, and

Towne House sheds and carriage house.

Towne House garden and summer house.

timber lands. He devoted much time to developing the farm on
which the house stood, raising sheep, improving cattle breeds,
experimenting with apple growing. He and his father were
typical gentleman farmers, even though farming with them was
a livelihood rather than a hobby.

The apple trees and the beautiful garden look out over the
millpond. The garden, laid out in beds radiating from a central
circle, has brick walks, a grape arbor, and a summer house. On
a clear day one can stand at its edge and look down on the
millpond and covered bridge, across to a tiny island, and see in
the quiet waters a reflection of the house and its surroundings.

Salem Towne's house was not unusual for its day and for
one of his social position, although he evidently considered it
something of a showpiece. It is simply the large, comfortable,
well-furnished house of a country magnate and gentleman
farmer. It is not essentially different from houses built by his
equals, but today its beauty is enhanced by the dignity of age,
the simple splendor of its gardens, and its site at the end of the
Village common, surrounded by and part of the physical remnants of the past. As such it takes on a new dimension and is
recognized as one of the loveliest survivals of late eighteenth-
century domestic architecture in New England.

Portrait of Moses Marcy (1777); from the Village art collection.

The Collections

So extensive and so varied were the collections of the two Wells brothers who founded Old Sturbridge Village that their holdings could not all be housed in the residences, shops, and other buildings. Thus the clock collection, the gun collection, the glass collection, and the lighting collection are displayed in structures outside the exhibition Village. The textile and art collections, still on the Green, will eventually be moved.

The Glass Exhibit

New Englanders imported their glass for windows, for table-wares, for mirrors, and for bottles and other containers until well into the nineteenth century, but they also made their own glass from the 1750's on. Early American glass was produced at the Germantown factory of Williams and Palmer before the Revolution; glass made by Robert Hewes at Temple, New Hampshire, and glass from the Pitkin factory in East Hartford was produced toward the close of that war. Following their lead were the Boston Crown Glass Company, the Mather Works in East Hartford, the Coventry Glass Works, the Willington Glass Company, the Marlboro Street Glass House of Keene, New Hampshire; the Boston Crown Glass Company, the New England Glass Company, the Boston & Sandwich Glass Company, and the Mount Washington Glass Works—all part of a thriving industry in this region.

The Old Sturbridge Village exhibit traces the development of New England glassmaking from the discovery in ancient times that sand, lead, and an alkali would fuse into a new material. The exhibit shows the ingredients that go into the making of glass as well as the techniques of blowing, mold-blowing, pressing, cutting, and etching. It shows some of the forms and varieties imported into New England, but devotes most of its space to the glass produced in the region.

One case shows some fine examples of New England blown glass—pitchers, decanters, and bowls—with a list of New England glass factories and their locations, dates of operation, and inventories of products. Three sections are devoted to bottles and flasks: English and American spirits bottles, chestnut and junk bottles, bottles bearing the labels of New England retailers, bitters bottles, and flasks made here and in other sections of the country. Then come an explanation and display of window glass—the chief product of the New England factories

English and Irish bar glasses.

—including cylinder glass and crown glass. Next are exhibits of looking glass, blown three-mold glass, pressed glass, drawer pulls, curtain ties, and knobs. There is a display of such practical objects as lamps, lanterns, thermometers, barometers, optical wares, and a microscope. The exhibition concludes with a display of some of the late art glass made in New England—Mary Gregory, Bohemian, peach blow, amberina, fuchsia, satin, and other varieties.

Outstanding in this exhibit is a section on paperweights that explains how these ultimate achievements of the glassblower's art are made and shows outstanding examples of French, English, and American weights of the nineteenth century. The fruit weights of the New England Glass Company and the flower and candy-cane weights of the Boston & Sandwich Glass Factory are especially impressive.

This exhibition is housed in a replica of the first American Optical Company building in Southbridge, Massachusetts.

The Gun Shop

The Harrington Gun Shop, an adaptation of an old building in Brookfield, Massachusetts, is a gambrel roof, story-and-a-half building with an ell in back and clapboarded on the outside. It contains the Village gun collection and an exhibit of wrought iron.

The gun collection covers the range of firearms used and made in New England. The earliest English settlers—who had to defend themselves against the Indians, occasionally against the French, and rarely against a Dutchman; who used their weapons for hunting, to secure food and skins; and who were required to train for the militia—had muskets and blunderbusses made in England, France, and Germany. By the time of the Revolution, however, desire and necessity pushed New England into production. Some of the earliest New England guns were of fine craftsmanship; more often they were poorly made and badly put together. But after the foundation of the new nation, with the impetus of the War of 1812, the Mexican War, and the opening of the Far West, American gunsmiths came into their own. Eli Whitney's experimentation with the manufacture of interchangeable parts made a revolution in the industry, and by the mid-nineteenth century New England gunsmiths were producing rifles, carbines, and pistols of every description. The evolution of this industry is shown in the gun collection.

Part of this exhibit is devoted to a display of militia accoutrements: uniforms, drums, spontoons, and the like. The size of this collection is still small but is constantly growing.

Behind the gun collection is the exhibit of wrought iron, which shows the development of the wrought-iron industry in New England from the earliest production at Saugus in the 1650's to 1840. The Saugus operation, which made both wrought and cast iron, soon went out of business, but by the opening of the nineteenth century half the iron and steel used in the United States was domestically produced, and New England was a leader in the industry. This exhibit explains what wrought iron is; where it came from; how it was made from bog and mined ore; how the charcoal pit, blast furnace, forge, and rolling and slitting mill were operated. Subsequent panels show the work of the New England blacksmith—his tools and techniques as well as his production in the form of horseshoes, cart tires, sleigh and wagon wheels, work for carriages and houses, axes, tongs, scythes, and repairs on guns and other hardware. At the far end of the exhibit is a collection that includes forged-iron tools, hardware, household equipment, and lighting devices.

The Clock Exhibit

The Village clock collection is housed in a little red brick replica of the schoolhouse of the Deneson District of Southbridge, Massachusetts, built about the time of the Civil War.

The collection consists of English-made clocks of the type that were imported into this country before the Revolution and those made by New England clockmakers. New Englanders had been leaders in the manufacture of parts and cases for these timepieces since the mid-eighteenth century. In the nineteenth century they applied their mechanical ability to producing clocks cheaply and captured the market in this country. Many

of the great names among New England clockmakers are represented here: Elnathan Taber; Simon, Aaron, and Benjamin Willard; Eli Terry; John Bailey; Gawen Brown; Lemuel Curtis;
and Caleb Wheaton. These men are represented by grandfather
clocks that are masterpieces of the cabinetmaker's as well as the
clockmaker's art; by grandmother clocks; by banjo, girandole,
lighthouse, pillar-and-scroll, and wagon-spring shelf clocks; and
by several wall clocks with pendulums. Many of these fine clocks
have beautifully painted dials and scenic panels; others have
delicately detailed inlay. The works are both wood and metal.
This is one of the finest existing collections of New England
timepieces. Anyone having the time to look it over carefully
will be impressed by the quality of workmanship these clocks
display—the precision of their mechanisms, the beauty of their
cases, and their fine tones as they strike the hour and half hour.
Just as they did a hundred years ago in most New England
farmhouses and shops, these clocks are still marking the hours
of our lives.

The Lighting Collection

Back in the early 1930's A. B. Wells seized on the oppor-
tunity to purchase in Switzerland the fine Dreyfus Collection
of lighting implements. This collection is the nucleus of the
present lighting collection on display in a small exhibition
building.

Here is told the story of lighting from ancient days to the
mid-nineteenth century. The terra-cotta and bronze pan-lamps
of ancient Greece and Rome; medieval rushlights and church
lights; bracket, spike, and standing candle holders of the six-
teenth and seventeenth centuries; and whale-oil and camphene
lamps, patent lamps, coach lanterns, glass candlesticks, and
lanterns of the type used in political rallies of the nineteenth
century are part of this wide-ranging collection. Ratchet holders, foot warmers, sconces, snuffers and extinguishers, and huge
standing branched candelabra complete the exhibition. Special
attention is given to the development of the Argand lamp,
which revolutionized lighting in the late eighteenth and early
nineteenth centuries. A shoemaker's reflecting globe is one of

the most interesting devices on exhibit. Taken as a whole, the display covers fairly comprehensively the story of artificial lighting before the age of gas and electricity.

Conclusion

Old Sturbridge Village:
The Present and the Past

The New England known to John Adams and John Quincy Adams, to John Hancock and Oliver Wolcott and Daniel Webster, to Hawthorne and Emerson and Thoreau, to Horace Mann and William Prescott and Jared Sparks, to John Warner Barber and William Matthew Prior, to Charles Chauncey and William Ellery Channing and Lyman Beecher is gone, beyond even the memory of any man now living. Its physical appearance is known to us in paintings and prints, its social, political, and intellectual life through the writings of its men of letters and of learning. These will remain even while the face of the countryside is changing beyond recognition and while even the New England most of us have known will be foreign to our children and grandchildren. How many of us have ever seen a liberty cap atop a liberty pole, a powder house, or an animal pound—or know what they existed for and what they meant? How many of our children will have ridden in a Pullman car or a Model A Ford, followed an ice wagon, or even have seen a circus parade through the Main Street of town? Civilization, social structure and customs, and even geography are changing so fast that one can only know what he himself sees and hears and feels and tastes and smells.

If the past of a nation is part of its present greatness, if individuals carry the genes of their ancestors, and if we—both as individuals and as a nation—are part of the long stream of

191

history, then it behooves us to learn and to understand something of our tradition and our heritage. Their story we are
taught in our homes, our schools, and our institutions of higher
learning. Part of that story, however, is purely physical, or
illusive, or based on memory without written records; it is hard
to teach and difficult to grasp.

Perhaps for this reason the outdoor museums, of which Old
Sturbridge Village is one, have a unique and important role to

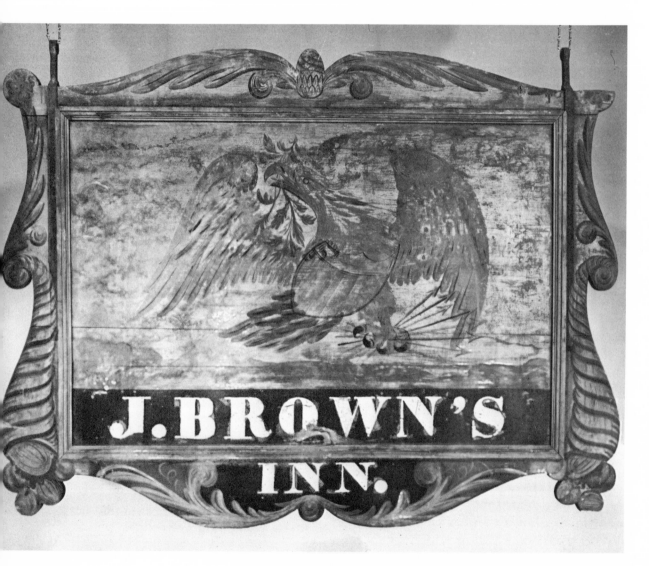

Sign at the Village Tavern.

play in the teaching of America's past and the transmission of
its heritage. They, as no other institution or individual, can provide us with the very sights and smells and sounds of the past. Surely to know by heart the Preamble to the Declaration of Independence and to realize what it meant in its day and in ours gives the individual a greater understanding of the past; but to have seen Independence Hall and the Mall brings a past reality within our grasp. To read about Jefferson and his contributions

Sign at the Village Boot Shop.

to politics, to science, and to the arts is to learn a great deal about his place in history, but to see his home, to examine the pieces of furniture he designed, to notice the hanging lamp he brought back from Paris, the gardens he laid out, the servants' quarters that housed the workers on his estate, is to know him more intimately and to have a new perspective on his age. The Adams House in Quincy reveals as no biography could the continuity of greatness that made up that family. Cooperstown shows us as no published text can the rural upstate New York of the mid-nineteenth century, and at Williamsburg we can feel the presence of the men who brought about the Revolution.

Doll, from the toy collection, Miner Grant's General Store.

It is in this sense that Old Sturbridge Village presents to us an aspect of rural New England in the early nineteenth century we cannot know by reading or by hearing. Here we can actually walk along a dusty (or muddy) country road, smell the fragrance of the orchards, and know that making and imbibing cider were farm practices until the temperance movement cut down the apple trees; here we can stop at the Pound to read the posted bylaw requiring the impounding of all stray horses, cattle, sheep, swine, and geese, and we can realize that fencing was as important to the New England farmer as it later was to become to his Western counterpart. We can peer into the Pow-

Squeak toy, from the toy collection, Miner Grant's General Store.

der House and realize that a yeomanry prepared to fight was necessary to a nation still dependent on Europe and regarded by that continent as little more than fair spoils. Along the Woodland Walk, as we see the trees and other plants known to every New Englander two centuries ago, we can begin to get a sense of the ecology and geology of the region.

The Stocks and Pillory near the Village Meetinghouse, largely relics of the past even to the early nineteenth century, tell us something of the story of local justice meted out by the justice of the peace nominated by the town and appointed by the legislature. The presence of barns and sheds by nearly every dwelling attest to the agricultural economy of the day. The chaise that drives past the Town House, the ox-cart on the farm road, and the pleasure wagon on the Green remind us that in an age before the presence of the automobile our ancestors walked, rode horseback, or, if they could afford it, traveled in the chaise, or coach, or wagon. Those of us who have seen on the screen only the covered wagons or the coaches that traveled the western routes get a glimpse of other modes of transportation. The Herb Barn and Garden show us the medicinal and common household plants known to housewives of long ago— those that could break a fever, cure a cold, ease a sore throat, dye a length of wool blue or russet or gold, make a facial or hand lotion, improve the complexion, or emphasize the red or gold in a fine head of hair.

We may also enter into the very spirit of politics or religion or philosophy of the day. In the Meetinghouse we may come

Boy on horse, from the toy collection, Miner Grant's General Store.

upon a dramatic reenactment that will reveal to us the appalling
hardships wrought by the system of poor relief, or poise us
between the economic necessities of the maritime states and of
the Federal government in the War of 1812, or enlist our sym-
pathies on the side of the courageous schoolmistress of Canterbury, Connecticut, who dared to admit Negro children to her
classroom, or show us the lure of the West as against the pull
of home ties, or the havoc wrought in home and community
by excessive drinking, or the plight of intelligent women who
had few, if any, rights in law. The problems and controversies,
the opposing points of view, and the perplexing moral, ethical,
political, and religious questions of early nineteenth-century
New England are here dramatically brought before us. We can
almost begin to delve beneath the skins of these people to see
why they believed and thought and acted as they did. Both the
dark side of the New England mind—its pessimism, its intol-

Wooden rocking horse, from the toy collection, Miner Grant's General Store.

erance, and its provincialism—and its deeply sensitive conscience are here revealed as no mere reading of history could uncover them.

A summer Punch and Judy Show enchants child visitors even as it sometimes horrifies their elders. The bloodthirstiness of Punch is often matched by that of his audience as it shrieks demands for the destruction of Judy and the animals. Connecticut's eighteenth-century legislation forbidding the production of this show at inns and taverns can well be understood after one has seen the performance itself.

In June comes the annual Militia Day, when marching bands of venerable military units parade on the Village Green. The Mattatuck Drum Band of Waterbury, Connecticut (oldest in this country), the New Haven Grays, and other ancient militia units take part in ceremonies that include the placing of the liberty cap, sacred to the Revolution, atop its pole, the posting of the Bill of Rights on the Meetinghouse Door, and the raising of the flag of 1795 of fifteen stars and stripes. All men of military age, except for clergymen and sometimes lawyers, were required to muster twice a year to train in the use of arms. The annual event at the Village commemorates the concept of a militia made up of freemen trained in the arts of defense.

Music is usually an important part of the heritage of any people, and thus the Village has a ballad singer on the Green every day and provides occasional concerts of music of the period. We can sit on a bench or on the grass along the Green and listen to the lovely old English and Scottish ballads handed down generation after generation; we can listen to these same tunes adapted to new American patriotic and folk themes; and we can trace a thread of new music coming from the church, the military, and the home alike. The more formal music of the ballroom, drawing room, and concert stage can be heard in occasional concerts at the Village Meetinghouse.

Other and unexpected residues of the past are there for us to see. In a room of the art exhibition a gentle-faced woman, seemingly a schoolmistress stepped out from one of the young ladies' seminaries of 1820, will be seen engaged in the genteel art of theorem painting, delicately painting on velvet a basket of flowers or fruit or some other conventional design of the early nineteenth century. In another gallery a young man will

Portrait of Mrs. John Forristall of Winchendon, Mass., by H. Bundy (1850);
from the Village art collection.

be intently working on his oil portrait of some member of the
staff; he is the descendant of the itinerant painters who wan-
dered up and down the New England countryside painting portraits for a living and who today are the "country" or "folk"
artists eagerly sought by collectors of Americana. In the Mashapaug House women can be observed spinning a fine linen or
woolen thread or weaving a coverlet, a rag carpet, or a web of

Portrait of Mrs. Chloe Allyn Sill and her infant son, by an unknown artist
(c. 1815); from the Village art collection.

toweling. By the time this book is off the press a cooper will be
hard at work in the farm cooperage turning out the barrels and
kegs so necessary to the New England farmer and housewife—
barrels for cider, fish, salt meat, flour, and other provisions,
kegs for nails and a hundred other items. Without these containers New England could not have exported along the coast
or to the Indies, nor could housewives have managed in their
kitchens and butteries.

All these exhibitions, demonstrations, and programs are the creation of a staff that has delved long and deeply into the New England scene. The role of the curatorial department in acquiring, cataloging, and exhibiting the collections has already been referred to. Whether the curator is purchasing a table made by a country cabinetmaker, cataloging an oil painting, or furnishing a room in a residence or in a shop, he must have at his command a knowledge both of the decorative and mechanical arts and of New England in the early nineteenth century. The information that makes up this body of knowledge is largely in the files of the research department, which in addition to undertaking detailed studies of subjects as diverse as town commons, New England medicine, the foods prepared and eaten by our ancestors, early transportation, town schooling, and agricultural crops, has incidentally amassed a whole corpus of miscellaneous information on funeral customs, window blinds, population movements, housecleaning, costumes, textiles, pewter making, fire fighting, forests, balloon ascensions, and poor relief in the early nineteenth century. In the research files one can find out what games were played in 1806, what styles of gowns women wore to an afternoon reception, what fabrics covered country sofas and chair seats, what New Englanders thought of divorce and of the servant problem. The Village music associate can give information about what was sung in the meetinghouses, what played at formal concerts and informal evening gatherings. The director of historical agriculture has made it his business to know how farms were fenced, what crops were grown, what kinds of sheep and cattle raised.

Close to hand is the Village library, which has a specialized collection of nearly 14,000 printed volumes as well as manuscripts and files of photographs, prints, films, and slides on various aspects of nineteenth-century New England. To the library comes the news bureau when it is working on a story of fireplace cooking; the crafts demonstration department, when it wants to know how a cartwheel was tired; the school services department, when it wishes to teach fourth graders to spin linen thread; the development department, when it gets a request for information on militia practices; the maintenance department, when it is planting a garden of early flowers; the membership

Portrait of Mrs. John Avery of Groton or Stonington, Conn., by an unknown
artist (c. 1785); from the Village art collection.

department, in answer to an inquiry on seventeenth-century
herbals; the merchandising department, when it is debating
whether or not to stock a reproduction of some eighteenth-
century piece of china. In a sense all members of the staff are
avid researchers, each digging into some aspect of the past in
order to present to Village visitors as authentic and as graphic
a picture of New England country life as is possible.

In all these many ways Old Sturbridge Village reflects the
past as no book or record could. It impinges on all the senses,
bringing to individuals of the twentieth century an illusion of a
civilization and a way of life that are our background and our
heritage.

Portrait of Allen Howland of West Brookfield and Worcester, Mass., by
Charles Curtis (1825); from the Village art collection.

Index

Abbott, John Radford, 108
Abington, Massachusetts, 47
Adams, John:
    on New England taverns, 85, 86-
      87, 94, 95-96, 98
    on New England villages, 16
    on office of justice of the peace, 81
    Stafford Springs, Conn., visited by,
      116
Adams, John Quincy, 71, 72, 79,
    104
Adams House (Quincy, Massachu-
    setts), 193
African Colonization Society, 49
Ainsworth, William F., 109
Alexander, Francis, 158, 174
Allen, William, 56
American Antiquarian Society, 127
American Optical Company, 4, 187
Ames, Fisher, 106
Amherst, New Hampshire, 103
Andover, Massachusetts, 57, 60
Anti-Slavery Society, 49
art exhibition, 184, 198, 199, 200,
    202, 203
Augusta, Maine, 18
Avery, John, 163

Avery, Mrs. John (Elizabeth), 163,
    202
Ayer, Sarah Connell, 107

Bailey, John, 189
Bailey, Sarah, 60
Bake House, 10, 12
Baldwin, Christopher Columbus:
    on New England law office, 82
    on New England taverns, 79, 96,
      100, 101, 102, 106
Baldwin, Roger Sherman, 70
Bangs, Edward, 123
Bank, Thompson, 118-123
banks, New England, 118-123
Baptist Meetinghouse, 10, 36
Baptists, in New England, 42-43
Barber, John Warner, 121
Barnard, Henry, 62
Bascom, Ruth Henshaw, 100, 101,
    107, 109
Beecher, Henry Ward, 57, 64
Beecher, Mrs. Lyman, 15
Belknap, Jeremy, 58, 100
Bentley, William, 48, 96
Berlin, Connecticut, 135
Beverly, Massachusetts, 45, 95

Birket, James, 105
blacksmiths, New England, 129-130, 188
Blacksmith Shop, 8, 10, 12, 128, 130
Blackstone, Sir William, 68, 76
Blashfield, Harvey, 120, 121
Boardman, David, 111
Bolton, Massachusetts, 10, 36, 130
boot shop, 8
Boston, Massachusetts:
    Latin School, 55
    school for the blind, 50
    taverns in, 90, 94, 103
Boudinot, Elias, 47, 48-49, 96, 99
Boy Scouts of America, 121
Braintree, Massachusetts, 48, 87
Brewster, John, 178
Brigham, Ephraim, 61
Brimfield, Massachusetts, 60
Bristol, Rhode Island, 58
Brookfield, Maine, 112
Brookfield, Massachusetts, 96, 98, 187
Brooks, Hervey, 136-137
Broommaker Shop, 135-136
Brown, Gawen, 189
Brunswick, Maine, 98
Brunton, Richard, 109
Bundy, Horace, 199
Burlington, Connecticut, 145

cabinetmakers, New England, 130
Cabinet Shop, 9, 130-132
Calhoun, John C., 70
Calvinism, 39
Camden, Maine, 100
Candia, New Hampshire, 53
candlemaker's shop, 10
candle-making demonstration, 165
Canterbury, Connecticut, 197
Canton, Massachusetts, 155
carding machines, in New England, 144-147
Carding mill, 7, 9, 10, 12, 138, 144-147
carriage house, 8

Chandler, Charles Church, 74
Channing, William Ellery, 150
Chapman, Asa, 72
Charlton, Massachusetts, 171, 180
Chastellux, Marquis de, 88, 92
Chauncey, Charles, 39
Chester, New Hampshire, 101
Clapp, Roger, 155
Clemence, Elliott, 6
Clock Exhibit, 9, 188-189
Coffin, Jacob, 103
Cogswell, Mason, 99
Coles, John, 109
Columbia College, 69
Comans, Sabra, see Towne, Mrs. Salem
Congregationalism, 38-40, 48, 50-51
conservator, 152
cooperage (cooper's shop), 11, 138, 200
Cooperstown, New York, 193
Covered Bridge, 4, 10
Crafts, Ebenezer, 97
Craftsbury, Vermont, 97
craftsmen, training of, 8
Crosby, Talcott, 121
curator, 9
curatorial department, 152
Curtis, Charles, 203
Curtis, Holbrook, 71-72
Curtis, Lemuel, 189

Danbury, Connecticut, 61
dancing, in taverns, 100-101
Danforth, John, 56
Davis, Eliakin, 82
Davis, Joseph H., 109
Davis, Simon, 121
Dedham, Massachusetts, 61, 106
deism, 43, 44, 45
demonstration building, 10
Denio, Aaron, 96-97
Dickinson, Levi, 136
Dilworth, Nicholas, 62
doctor's office, 11
Doyle, Margaret B., 163-164

Dublin, New Hampshire, 57
Dudley, John, 75-76
Dudley, Massachusetts, 56
Dummerston, Vermont, 11
Dunstable, Massachusetts, 61
Dunstable, New Hampshire, 102
Durham, Connecticut, 93, 153
Duxbury, Massachusetts, 97
Dwight, Timothy, 13, 88, 98, 99

East Brookfield, Massachusetts, 8, 167
East Hartford, Connecticut, 185
education in New England, 53-64
Edwards, Jonathan, 39, 49
Ellsworth, William W., 70
Emerson, Ralph Waldo, 99, 106
Episcopal Church, 38, 42
Evans, Oliver, 141

Fairbanks, Josiah, 113
Fairfield, Connecticut, 54
Farmhouse, Freeman, 10, 21-33
Farmington, Connecticut, 101
Farmington, Maine, 59
farms, New England, 19-33
Fenno, Isaac, 155
Fenno, John, 154, 155
Fenno House, 10, 148, 150, 154,
    155-159, 165, 171
Field, Erastus Salisbury, 109
Fisher, William, 121
Fish House, New York, 108
Fiskdale, Massachusetts, 10, 36
Fitch, Erastus, 162
Fitch, Jesse, 162
Fitch, Stephen, 109, 154, 162
Fitch, Mrs. Stephen, 162
Fitch, Stephen, Jr., 162
Fitchburg, Massachusetts, 82
Fitch House, 150, 153, *160-166*,
    171
flood (1955), 10, 22
Forristall, Mrs. John, *199*
Fowle, Daniel, 125
Franklin, Benjamin, 39
Franklin Primer, 62

Freeman, Comfort, 21
Freeman, Pliny, 21
Freeman Farm, 10, 21-33
fulling mill, 138

Gate House, 7, 8
Gay, Joseph D., 121
General Store, Miner Grant's, 112,
    114, 115, 116-118, 123
general stores, in New England, 111-
    118
Gilead, Connecticut, 8, 142
Glass Exhibit, 185-187
Gloucester, Massachusetts, 55
Goodrich, Ebenezer, 178
Goodrich, Samuel, 48, 105-106
Goshen, Connecticut, 49, 100, 136
Gould, James, 70
Grant, Billings, 116, 117
Grant, Miner, 116-117
Grant, Miner, Jr., 116-117
graveyard, 36, 51
Great Awakening, 39, 45, 49
Green, the, xii, 8, 10, 108, 150
Greenfield, Massachusetts, 56, 97
Greenleaf, Benjamin, 109
Gristmill, Village, 8, 11, 118, 139-
    142, 147
gristmills, in New England, 138-142
Grosvenor, Robert, 120
Groton, Massachusetts, 91
Grund, Francis J., 94
Gun Shop, 8, 187

Hale, Edward Everett, 103
Halfway Covenant, 38, 39
Hall, Mrs. Basil, 91
Hamilton, Dr. Alexander, 92
Handcraft House, 10
Hapgood, Oliver, 144
Hartford, Connecticut:
    deaf and dumb, school for, 50
    insane, hospital for, 50
    Latin school, 54
Hartford, Connecticut (*cont.*)
    taverns, 101, 102, 103
    tinsmith, 135

Harvard, Massachusetts, 48, 105
Harvard College, 54, 55, 66, 70
Hawthorne, Nathaniel, 106
Hebron, Connecticut, 8, 139
Henshaw, Ruth, *see* Bascom, Ruth Henshaw
Henshaw, William, 101
Herb Barn and Garden, 10, 196
Hewes, Robert, 185
History of Printing in America (Thomas), 127
Hitchcock, Apollos, 103
Hitchcock, Enos, 154
Holley, Helen G., 160
Hopkinton Springs, Massachusetts, 101
houses, New England, 149-183
Howland, Southworth Allen, 164, 203
Howland, Mrs. Southworth Allen, 164
humanitarianism, in New England, 1-2, 49-50
Huntington, Samuel (nephew of governor), 73-74, 77
Huntington, Governor Samuel (Connecticut), 62, 73
Hutchinson, Thomas, 1
Hyde family, 117

Inns of Court, London, 66, 68

Jaffrey, New Hampshire, 116
Jefferson, Thomas, 44, 193

Keeler, Timothy, 97
Keene, New Hampshire, 100, 185
Kettel, Russell, 6
Killingly, Connecticut, 119
King, James, 69
Knight, Sarah, 92

Lafayette, General, 91, 109, 164
Lancaster, New Hampshire, 145
Langley, Eli, 97
Larcom, Lucy, 95
Law Office, 67, 72, 74-75, 77

lawyers, New England, 65-83
Leicester, Massachusetts, 100
Lexington, Massachusetts, 59
Lighting Collection, 189-190
Lincoln House, 10
Litchfield, Connecticut, 15, 70, 76, 79, 100, 145
  courthouse, 76, 79
  dame school, 57
  female seminary, 70, 100
  law school, 70
Little, William, 105
Londonderry, New Hampshire, 103
Long, Zadoc, 94, 99
Loring, Lucius, 112-113
Lothrop, Daniel, 61
Lyman, Eliphalet, 72

McClellan, John, 72-83, 150, 153
McClellan, Mrs. John (Faith Williams), 74
McIntire, Samuel, 110
Magnolia, Massachusetts, 100, 101
maintenance department, 152
Manchester, New Hampshire, 58
Mann, Horace, 150
Mansfield, Connecticut, 164
Marcy, Moses, 184
Marlboro, Massachusetts, 61, 94
Marsh, Isaac, 102
Martin, Joseph Plumb, 95
Martin, Marcus, 70
Martineau, Harriet, 89, 91, 95, 107, 154
Mashapaug, Connecticut, 108
Mashapaug House, 10, 199
Mason, William H., 120
Massachusetts Spy (newspaper), 125, 126
Mather, Cotton, 56, 58, 159
meetinghouse:
  Quaker, 10, 34, 36
  Village (Baptist), 10, 36, 37, *46*, 195, 196, 198
meetinghouses, New England, 35-51, 85, 88

Melish, John, 158
Mendon, Massachusetts, 59
Meriden, Connecticut, 135
Methodism, in New England, 43
Milford, Connecticut, 87, 99
Militia Day, 198
millpond, 8, 10
Milton, Massachusetts, 138
Montague, Massachusetts, 96
Montville, Connecticut, 145
Morse, Jedidiah, 62
music, 198

Natick, Massachusetts, 55
New Bedford, Massachusetts, 15
Newburyport, Massachusetts, 79, 103, 104
New Divinity men, 44
New England Primer, 62
New Haven, Connecticut:
  green, 14
  hotel, 102
  militia unit, 198
  schools, 54
  taverns, 92, 99
New London, Connecticut, 54, 73, 102
New Milford, Connecticut, 111
Newell, Daniel Fiske, 158
Newport, Rhode Island, 61
Nichols, John, 120
Nichols, Jonathan, 121
Norfolk, Connecticut, 45
Northampton, Massachusetts, 39, 136
Northfield, Massachusetts, 59
Norwalk, Connecticut, 109
Norwich, Connecticut, 61, 73, 81, 100
Nott, Samuel, 103

Old Cheney Mill (Gilead, Connecticut), 142
Old Lyme, Connecticut, 58, 153
Old Sturbridge Inc. 8
Osborne, John, 108
Oxford, Massachusetts, 179

Pain, William, 171
Paine, Thomas, 44, 45
paperweights, 187
Paris Hill, Maine, 79
Parker, Isaac, 56
Parkman, Ebenezer, 93-94
Parrish, John, 78
Parsons, Theophilus, 71, 75
Peabody, Steven, 94
Peter the Great, 66
Pettes, Samuel, 79
Pewterer's Shop, 132-133
Philadelphia, College of, 69
Pierce, Thomas, 164
Pike, Nicholas, 62
Pilgrims, 38
Pittsfield, Massachusetts, 145
Pittsfield, New Hampshire, 17
Plymouth, Massachusetts, 61, 95
Porter Gristmill (Hebron, Connecticut), 139
Portsmouth, New Hampshire, 55, 105, 125, 153
Pottery Shop, 10, 136-137
Pound, 10, 194
Powder House, 10, 194-195
Priestley, Joseph, 44
Prince, Hezekiah, 100, 101, 102
Printing Office, 10, 12, 123-127
Prior, William Matthew, 109
Protestantism, in New England, 35-51
Providence, Rhode Island, 47
Pug Mill, 136
Punch and Judy Show, 198
puppet show, 11
Puritans and Puritanism, 38, 49, 51, 54
Putnam, Connecticut, 121

Quaker Meetinghouse, 10, 34, 36
Quakers, in New England, 43
Quincy, Massachusetts, 193
Quinebaug River, 3, 8, 21
Quinabaug Village Corporation, 8

INDEX

210

Reading, Massachusetts, 45
Reed, William, 121
Reeve, Tapping, 70, 76
religion, in New England, 38-51
research department, 152
residences, New England, 149-183
Revere, Paul, 158
Rice, Albert W., 144
Richardson, Solomon, 154, 167
Richardson House, 150, 153, 154, 165, 167-171
Ridgefield, Connecticut, 59, 97
Riznik, Barnes, 146
Robbins, Philemon, 57
Rochefoucault-Liancourt, Duc de la, 80, 83, 98, 105, 116
Rowley, Massachusetts, 47
Ryefield, Massachusetts, 90

Salem, Massachusetts, 55, 103
Salem, New Hampshire, 59
Saugus, Massachusetts, 187
Sawmill, Village, 8, 138, 142, *143*, 147
sawmills, in New England, 143
Saybrook Platform, 38, 39
Schaefer, R. J., Foundation, 109
Schipper, Gerrit, 109
Schoharie, New York, 8
Scholfield, Arthur, 144
Scholfield, John, 144
Schoolhouse, 52, 53-54, 63, 64
schools, New England, 53-64
Seabury, Samuel, 42
Second Great Awakening, 45
Seymour, Mabel, 76
Shakers, 43
Sharon, Connecticut, 76
Shays' Rebellion, 67
Sheffield, Massachusetts, 88
Sherman, Roger Minot, 154
Shirley, Massachusetts, 48
Shute, R. W., 109
Shute, S. A., 109
Sill, Mrs. Chloe Allyn, 200
Simsbury, Connecticut, 47, 106

Skillin, Simeon, Jr., 110
sleighing parties, 100, 106
Slosson, Barzillai, 76
Smith, Hoe & Company, 126
Smith, John Cotton, 76
Smith, Moses, 109
Society for the Preservation of New England Antiquities, 125, 153
Southbridge, Massachusetts, 4, 21, 187, 188
Southington, Connecticut, 47
South Waterford, Maine, 144
Spaulding-Potter Charitable Trust (Concord, New Hampshire), 53
spectacle shop, 8
Springfield, Massachusetts, 61
Stafford, Connecticut, 8, 116-117
Stafford Springs, Connecticut, 116
Starr, Comfort, 61
Sterling, Massachusetts, 113
Stiles, Ezra, 72
Stobbs, George R., 74
stores, general, in New England, 111-118
Stoughton, Israel, 138
Stoughton, Massachusetts, 155
Stowe, Harriet Beecher, 16, 154
Strong, Eleanor, *see* Fitch, Mrs. Stephen
Sturbridge, Massachusetts, 90, 97, 162
Sutton, Massachusetts, 97

Taber, Elnathan, 189
Tavern, Village, 10, 84, 88, 89, 93, 107-110, 192-193
taverns, New England, 85, 162
teachers, New England, 64
Temple, New Hampshire, 185
Terry, Eli, 189
textile exhibition, 10
textile mill, 11
Thackara, William Ward, 90, 96
Thomas, Isaiah, 123-127
Thomaston, Maine, 102
Thompson, Connecticut, 119-121

tinplate industry, 133-135
Tinsmith Shop, 7-8, 133-135
Tisbury, Massachusetts, 90, 96
Tolland, Connecticut, 111
Towne, Salem, 150, 154, 171, 172, 175, 179-183
Towne, Mrs. Salem, 151, 152, 180
Towne, Salem, Jr., 174, 179, 181-182
Towne House, 150, 152, 153, 154, 171-*183*
toy collection, 194-197
Transylvania University (Kentucky), 69
Trumbull, Jonathan, 74
turkey shoots, 101

Unitarianism, 45

villages, New England, 13-18

Waldoboro, Maine, 11
Walpole, Massachusetts, 82
Wansey, Henry, 14, 92, 98
Washington, George, 87, 91, 109, 110
Waterbury, Connecticut, 198
Waterford, Maine, 97
Waterford, Vermont, 94
Wells, Albert Bacheller, 4-6, 8, 108, 185, 189
Wells, Ethel Burnham, 6
Wells, George Burnham, 6
Wells, Joel Cheney, 4, 8, 10, 171, 185
Wells, Marion Hengerer, 10, 171
Wells Historical Museum, 8
Wendell, Oliver, 107
Westboro, Massachusetts, 101
West Lebanon, New Hampshire, 36

Westminster, Massachusetts, 41
West Simsbury, Connecticut, 45
Weymouth, Massachusetts, 94, 99
Wheaton, Caleb, 189
White, Ezra, 117
Wight House, 7, 8
Wilder, Abraham, 130
Wilder, Moses, 130
Willard, Aaron, 189
Willard, Benjamin, 189
Willard, Emma, 62
Willard, Samuel, 116
Willard, Simon, 122
William and Mary College, 69
Williams, Faith, *see* McClellan, Mrs. John
Williams, Steven, 72
Williams, William, 74
Williamsburg, Virginia, 193
Willimantic, Connecticut, 8, 160
Wilson, James, 69
Winchester, New Hampshire, 36
Windham, Connecticut, 160-161
Windsor, Connecticut, 94
Winslow, Isaac, 77
Winslow, Mrs. Sarah, 61
Woodbridge, William C., 62
Woodbury, Levi, 70
Woodland Walk, 5, 195
Woodstock, Connecticut, 72, 74, 80, 81, 92
woodworking shop, 7
Worcester, Massachusetts, 103, 123-124, 150
Wright, Frances, 81, 99
Wrought Iron Exhibit, 188

Yale College, 70, 72, 74, 75, 76, 88
York, Maine, 79
Young Millwright's Guide (Evans), 141